First Edition

THE LITTLE BLACK BOOK OF LYING BORIS JOHNSON

—

From journalist to prime minister, how
one man's lies re-shaped modern Britain.

Kyle Taylor

With:

Introduction by Hardeep Matharu

Foreword by Dawn Butler MP

Afterword by Peter Stefanovic

BYLINE
BOOKS

LONDON, UNITED KINGDOM

Byline Books

London, United Kingdom

First published in the United Kingdom of Great Britain
and Northern Ireland by Byline Books, 2022

Text copyright © Dawn Butler, Peter Stefanovic
and Kyle Taylor, 2022

Cover design by Steve Leard

Layout by Prepare to Publish

Printed in Great Britain by Short Run Press Ltd

ISBN UK: 978-1-8384629-4-9

*To every person whose life has been
irreparably harmed by Boris Johnson.*

CONTENTS

—

INTRODUCTION:
A MOMENT IN TIME

—

BY HARDEEP MATHARU

One moment in time can sometimes encapsulate the fundamentals of a problem looming so large that it is otherwise difficult to grasp.

When the Labour MP, and author of the foreword of this book, Dawn Butler was asked to leave the House of Commons in 2021, after calling Boris Johnson a "liar", the system exposed how broken it is. How is it that a Prime Minister can repeatedly lie and make misleading statements at the despatch box without reproach, while those who call this out are punished? Such a system is vulnerable. It is also dangerous.

The Johnson era showed us, like none before it, that Britain's unwritten constitution – reliant on norms and conventions and 'good chaps' who will exercise power honourably – is no longer fit for purpose faced with those unwilling to play by the rules. When Dawn Butler left the chamber that day, she revealed the absurdity of the situation we're in.

But the urgency required to tackle these constitutional failings is lacking – with the absence of a truly robust and independent free press, upholding its democratic duty as the 'fourth estate', only adding to our problems. In Britain, it is predominantly the private interests of wealthy media proprietors which are advanced, in partnership with their political allies, rather than the public interest. Even the BBC, once renowned for its trustworthiness, has failed to hold politicians to account amidst a backdrop of rising populist politics.

These institutional failings, which have always been the undercurrent, were exposed by the impact of the campaign to leave the EU. The way in which the Brexit project was advanced by Boris Johnson's Vote Leave group and others fundamentally altered the water we swim in. It normalised behaviour that should not be normalised. It allowed those meant to be representing the public to lie and stoke fear in the name of the 'will of the people'.

This has now morphed into a 'hypernormalisation' within British politics; a state of affairs in which the public and the politicians know those in power are engaged in obfuscation – but no change seems available.

As thousands of people died isolated around us, Johnson's then chief advisor Dominic Cummings sat in the Downing Street rose garden telling people he drove to Barnard Castle to test his eyesight. Cabinet ministers, and Johnson himself, lined up to tour radio and television stations to support his claims that betrayed such contempt for this country's people. Many, many other instances followed during the pandemic when it was clear to us, the public, that our politicians were not being straight with the country. The cost came in lives lost.

In their refusal to engage with the realities of Brexit and Britain's post-imperial identity crisis, large swathes of our political-media class continue this contamination of our politics now.

If we cannot go back, how do we move forward? While we wait for institutional reforms, we can start with ourselves – by understanding how we ended up here. By challenging ourselves to really confront what the new 'normal' says about the country Britain has been, and is, we can arm ourselves with the tools to fight against it.

There's no better place to start than the *Little Black Book of Lying Boris Johnson.*

Hardeep Matharu is a journalist and the Editor of *Byline Times*

FOREWORD:
LIARS GONNA LIE

—

BY DAWN BUTLER MP

The UK is sleepwalking into authoritarianism. It often feels like there's not a lot you can do when your main opposition has been in power so long. It's easy to feel powerless.

While Brexit was a turning point, for me the moment of realising total powerlessness was when Boris Johnson unlawfully prorogued Parliament. It was an assault on democracy, which we have fought hard for. People literally died for the vote. In the UK, it has always been easier to lose than gain. Our rights are not enshrined in a codified constitution that is irrevocable but in customs and norms, the most important of which is primacy of Parliament. When the Prime Minister wanted to shut down Parliament, what he was really trying to do was shut down democracy.

When Boris Johnson's attempt to do this was overturned by the Supreme Court, the next thing for him was to go for the judges – that *Daily Mail* headline still haunts me: "Enemies of the People".

Johnson was clearly showing his true colours and it was happening in plain sight right in front of us. It felt like *The Handmaid's Tale* had come to life!

That moment felt like my rock bottom. I couldn't imagine things getting any worse. This is why I called the then Prime Minister a liar on the floor of the House of Commons. I felt that I had to do something, whatever I could, to draw attention to what was going on.

It happened when I was taking part in a "summer adjournment" debate just before the end of business for the day, shortly before the end of the final day of all business before the summer recess in 2021. I said that poor people in this country had paid with their lives because Boris Johnson had spent the last 18 months misleading the House and the country.

I cited Peter Stefanovic's video of Johnson's lies that has been viewed by 40 million people. I was especially incensed by Boris's assertion that the vaccination programme had "severed" the link between infection and serious illness and death. This lie gave people the impression that, once vaccinated, you could carry on without caution, which just was not true. I said that he should come to the House and correct the fact that he had lied about this over and over again.

The stand-in Deputy Speaker asked me twice to withdraw my assertion that the Prime Minister had lied. Despite feeling incredibly nervous at that moment, I refused and was suspended for the rest of the parliamentary sitting. It was a necessary sacrifice to call out his behaviour. I believe that, as elected representatives, we have a duty to the public to be honest and accurate – and be even more careful to do so in times of upheaval or a worldwide emergency such as the COVID pandemic.

I had to leave the chamber and it had been made official: the outdated rules mean you can lie to the House with impunity but you can't tell the truth about the fact that someone has lied. This fact continues to baffle me and I imagine many people across the country too.

I didn't expect to have to leave the chamber and the House. Interestingly, some of the members on the government benches completely understood why I had done it. They didn't want the system to be corrupted and many came up to me to share their appreciation for my having taken a stand.

What did surprise me was the lack of support I got from my own side. I was largely shunned, even though it had taken great courage to do what I did, holding the Prime Minister and the government to account, which is the literal job of the Opposition. While most in the Labour Party seemed to have just ignored what I had done, the public was much more supportive. The video of me accusing the then Prime

Minister of lying has more than 5 million views and I am still getting letters of support today, even after he is gone. But at the time of writing, he had just worryingly threatened a comeback as leader of the Conservatives and Prime Minister. This won't be his last attempt.

We must never forget the damage Boris Johnson has done to our democracy; he has seriously undermined parliamentary procedures, which have been built and developed over time and rely on decent honourable behaviour in the House of Commons.

Boris Johnson seems to have only one thing on his mind: himself. As we watch with horror at Liz Truss's government further dismantling everything we hold dear, we cannot and should not forget that Boris Johnson will do absolutely anything to get himself back into power. That's why Peter, Kyle and I felt a need to put together a first volume (there could be so many) of the most egregious lies Boris Johnson has told. We can't allow him to rewrite his own history over time and we absolutely can't allow him anywhere near power ever again. Let this be a factual record and a warning that liars are always gonna lie.

As for what happened to me, Boris never did correct the record about the word "severed", which was patently and scientifically untrue. He also failed to correct the record on many of the other issues I raised, such as on the economy. Still, I believe what I did was important and in some ways I started an important conversation about Boris Johnson's conduct. I sincerely hope it had an impact on the public perception of Johnson. My job as a public servant is to look after my constituents by holding power to account and I will never stop fighting.

PART 1

THE RISE OF A
PROFESSIONAL LIAR

BORIS THE LYING JOURNALIST

From the very beginning of his career, Boris Johnson was a proven liar. Looking back on his rise from a journalist to Mayor of London before being the public face of the Brexit campaign, the pattern of habitual dishonesty and disregard for the truth is obvious. Though his early lies potentially weren't as harmful as those he told from Number 10, they help characterise a man totally unable to tell the truth.

JOHNSON'S FIRST LIE

You don't have to look far into Boris Johnson's career before his lies start rearing their ugly head. Just one year after graduating from Oxford University, he was fired from his first job at *The Times* for making up a quote.

In a front-page article, Johnson wrote about the archaeological discovery of Edward II's Rose Palace.[1] The only problem was that Johnson didn't know much about Edward II beyond his rumoured relationship with his lover Piers Gaveston. To help with the article he called his godfather and Oxford history professor, Colin Lucas.[2] Despite being an expert on a totally different subject – the French Revolution – Lucas dutifully provided Johnson with some quotes for his article. Upon publication Lucas was nonetheless still shocked to find himself being misquoted as having said that Edward II and Gaveston conducted their affair at Rose Palace.[3]

The only small problem with this invention from Johnson was that Gaveston had been beheaded a dozen years before the palace was built. This lie not only damaged the reputation of his paper. Johnson's godfather also suffered a hit to his reputation and failed to become Master of Balliol College. Since this incident Boris claims to have felt "a deep, deep sense of shame and guilt" over it [4] but, fear not, this didn't stop him writing a follow-up piece on the exact same topic. Furthermore, according to some people, when his contract with *The Times* was terminated over the lies, Boris claimed *The Times*, considered a paper of record, made up most of their quotes anyway.[5]

LYING ABOUT EU COFFIN SIZES

In 2004, long before the Brexit campaign began, Boris was already taking part in one of his most beloved pastimes –spreading misinformation about the European Union. In his 2003 book *Lend Me Your*

Ears Johnson claimed that one of the most outrageous pieces of EU regulatory overreach into British life was how it dictated regulations around size and shape of coffins.[1]

Of course, this is a complete lie. No regulation remotely like this exists. If you were being generous, you could maybe point to the 1973 Agreement on the Transfer of Corpses. However, this didn't come from the EU. It came as a convention from the Council of Europe of which the UK is not a signatory, so it has no standing in UK law.[2]Regardless, even that is just a treaty designed to set minimum safety standards for coffins used to transport corpses. It doesn't set size or shape limits.[3]

Of course, it being clearly untrue hasn't stopped Johnson repeating the lie time and time again. When questioned about it at a select committee in 2016 he again claimed there were "Euro Coffin" regulations.[4] The then Chairman of the Treasury Select Committee Andrew Tyrie told him they were a "figment of his imagination" and that Boris's blundering response to this was merely him "busking".[5]

Although hardly his worst, this lie set a pattern of Boris's near psychotic pattern of spreading falsehoods about the European Union as a journalist, a mayor, a Brexit campaigner, a Foreign Secretary, and a Prime Minister. This type of misinformation, spread a decade before the referendum was even held, profoundly poisoned the well of the British public's trust in the EU, setting the stage for bigger lies about the EU that were also believed by the public.

LYING ABOUT THE HILLSBOROUGH TRAGEDY

During his time as Editor of the *Spectator* one of the many inflammatory pieces Boris published was an editorial claiming that Liverpool refused to accept the role that drunk fans played in the Hillsborough Stadium tragedy in 1989, in which 97 football supporter died in a human crush.[1]

The article was rightly met with a great deal of backlash and Johnson felt the need to respond to this in what he called "Operation Scouse-grovel" the following week.[2] However, far from walking back the claims that Liverpool was "hooked on grief", Johnson went further in his follow-up piece, claiming that we can be "authors of our misfortunes", which was a pretty clear inference to Liverpool fans' own responsibility for the tragedy.[3]

Apart from being insulting to the victims and their families specifically and the City of Liverpool generally, as a whole the article was a complete lie. The Hillsborough inquest concluded drunk fans were not responsible for what happened that day, and that the crowd had actually been far more sober than police officers had accounted for.[4] Johnson briefly apologised for the editorial, admitting it was incorrect in 2012.[5]

This lie helped keep alive the false narrative of the Liverpool fans being to blame for Hillsborough and was insulting to the Hillsborough victims and their loved ones. As Prime Minister, Boris has repeatedly refused to apologise to the people of Liverpool.[6]

BORIS THE LYING POLITICIAN

—

SACKED FOR LYING (AGAIN)

In 2004, Johnson's habit of lying to his employers came back to bite him when he was fired for the second time in his career by Conservative Party leader Michael Howard. The reason? You guessed it. Lying to him.[1]

Johnson had been accused of having an affair with another journalist named Petronella Wyatt. She was Deputy Editor of the *Spectator* when Johnson was originally appointed Editor and rumours had swelled about the couple. Johnson denied them as an "inverted pyramid of piffle".[2] He directly told Michael Howard the same to his face. So when it came out that Johnson had been lying the whole time, Howard asked Johnson to resign. He of course refused, likely believing, as ever, that rules did not apply to him. As a result, Howard was forced to fire him instead, a moment which the *Guardian* claimed at the time had brought Johnson's political career to an end.[3] If only. The fact that being sacked twice over lying didn't disqualify Johnson from all the later higher offices he held raises serious questions about the broader state of British politics.

LYING TO HIS BOSS (AGAIN)

Conrad Black, the former owner of the *Spectator* and *Telegraph*, learnt the hard way what so many people have since learnt: You can't trust Boris Johnson. Before Black made Boris the Editor of the *Spectator* magazine, Johnson promised him he would give up on his political career[1] and wouldn't run for parliament while he was working at the *Spectator*. Having been made the magazine's Editor in 1999, Johnson didn't wait long to break this promise. He was selected as the Conservative candidate for the seat of Henley ahead of the 2001 General Election.

While at a hustings to be their prospective candidate, Johnson had also promised the Conservative Association of Henley that, were he to become an MP, he would quit as Editor of the *Spectator*.[2] You'll be shocked to learn he lied to them as well. At this point, Boris was running two competing lies against each other, a skill he would continue to hone in the years to come.

Johnson ended up staying on as Editor of the *Spectator* until 2005, despite winning his seat in 2001. On top of these two jobs (to both of which he promised to quit the other), Johnson had a third gig writing a *Telegraph* column and a fourth gig writing regular motoring columns for *GQ* magazine. Don't worry, he did all of these jobs marvellously, if by marvellously we mean not at all. Which job got the least attention, you ask? The one that was paid for by you, the taxpayer. Johnson only attended just over half of all parliamentary votes.[3]

This wasn't the only time Johnson lied about not taking on multiple jobs. According to the *New Statesman*, Johnson lied at least 17 times by saying he wouldn't run as an MP while being Mayor of London, which he did in 2015.[4]

So, it should come as no surprise that throughout his long career Johnson repeatedly misled when saying he had no desire to be Prime Minister. In 2012 when asked if he wanted to be Prime Minister, in perhaps his most bald-faced lie ever, Johnson simply replied, "No – of course not".[5]

LYING ABOUT THE GARDEN BRIDGE

The Garden Bridge is a signature failure of Boris Johnson's career, and the project's history is littered with lies. Initially conceived as a pedestrian footbridge over the Thames full of wildlife and greenery [1], the bridge was promised as a "gift to the people of London".[2] Boris went on to claim in November 2013 that it would be the Trustees of the Garden Bridge and not the part publicly funded Transport for London (TfL) that would put together the funding for it. None of this turned out to be true and just two months later it was revealed that the total public cost would be £60 million.[3]

The most controversial part of the development of the project came when the Trust awarded a £21 million contract to a construction company before obtaining planning permission for the project.[4] A report by the Greater London Assembly (GLA), the legislative branch of London's government, called this a reckless decision and directly criticised Johnson for his role in pressuring TfL to "downplay" the big risks involved with the project throughout its development.[5]

Even after the project's complete collapse, Johnson continued to dodge responsibility and lie about the project. Appearing in front of the GLA, he claimed the bridge "had received every relevant planning permission" when in fact it had yet to finalise any deal with Westminster or Lambeth Council, as both were dependent upon a guarantee that the Mayor's office would pay for maintenance of the bridge.[6] Perhaps the biggest lie Johnson told about the Garden Bridge came during his appearance in front of the GLA in 2018, when he claimed he didn't waste "a single penny" [7] of taxpayers' money.

In fact, the project, which did not lead to a bridge of any kind whatsoever, wasted £43 million of public money.[8] That's your money he wasted.

LYING ABOUT HIS CRONYISM

In 2010, details emerged of an alleged affair between Boris Johnson and an unpaid City Hall adviser named Helen Macintyre.[1] This was specifically a problem as Ms Macintyre had been appointed by Johnson to an unofficial role, with no scrutiny of her appointment from the GLA.[2] Furthermore, Johnson hadn't disclosed their relationship, and this deceit put him in breach of the rules of City Hall.He was found to have committed a "technical breach of the code of conduct" by the GLA's assessment subcommittee.[3]

You'd think Johnson would have learnt his lesson from this. You'd have thought wrong. Just a few years later, he proceeded to do almost the exact same thing with US businesswoman Jennifer Arcuri. While the two were having an affair, Johnson gave Arcuri's business £126,000 of public money through grants and sponsorship.[4] As if that wasn't enough, Arcuri also accompanied Johnson on three foreign trade missions.[5] At least one of these received public funding, which an official GLA report into the matter concluded Arcuri had benefited indirectly from.[6]

Not only is this an example of straightforward cronyism, it also shows just how shameless Johnson is, taking the public, who once again were funding his salary as mayor, for absolute mugs.

LYING ABOUT LONDON'S CHALLENGES

When Johnson wasn't breaking manifesto pledges or coming up with ridiculous vanity projects, he was supposedly running London as its mayor. However, to cover for his lacklustre efforts he often resorted to lying about the problems the city was facing, because there's no need to solve a problem that doesn't exist.

For example, in 2012 Johnson claimed that the casualty rate for London cyclists had gone down.[1] He was quickly corrected on this by Jenny Jones, a member of the London Assembly for the Green Party. When looking at journeys made on all of London's roads, the casualty rate *increased* after Johnson took office in 2008.[2] Johnson also tried to claim that it is often the fault of reckless cyclists that accidents occur [3], yet a report by the Department for Transport found this was only a contributing factor in 2% of cases.[4] Still, denying a problem exists and blaming the victims is a tried and tested way of avoiding responsibility for Boris.

Johnson also dodged responsibility on climate change. He ran for the mayoralty claiming he wanted to "go greener and cleaner" in London.[5] Yet once mayor, he promoted the conspiracy theorist Piers Corbyn, claiming his weather forecasts were more accurate than those of the Met Office.[6] Johnson even went so far as to claim Planet Earth is heading for a "mini Ice Age".[7] Once more, pretending a problem didn't exist gave Johnson an excellent excuse to do nothing.

Why work when you can take credit for imaginary policies, like claiming to have put £445 in the pockets of Londoners? [8] This figure, a completely invented amount, was supposedly the sum of money Ken Livingstone would have raised council tax by had he beaten Johnson.[9] This wasn't based on any published plans of Livingstone but instead concocted by taking the average of Livingstone's previous council tax rises, which were of course unrelated to the claim.

Johnson's tenure as mayor was riddled with lies. He consistently downplayed problems to avoid taking responsibility for dealing with them, instead claiming to have solved imaginary ones. As a result, one of the world's major cities was left with a leader prattling on about another ice age instead of dealing with the impending climate disaster.

LYING ABOUT MAKING PROMISES

Politicians are often accused of making promises they won't deliver on in order to get elected. Johnson raised this to an art form. Unfortunately, there isn't time to catalogue every promise Johnson lied about when running for mayor, but here are a few of the worst.

LYING ABOUT TUBE STATION TICKET OFFICES

One of the most brazen examples of Johnson's deception has to be his saying that he would keep a ticket office open at every tube station that already had one.[1] Johnson not only went back on this promise but completely U-turned, announcing five years later that almost all ticket offices would close by 2016.[2] This broken promise cost 900 people their jobs, all of whom had been promised by Johnson that no such change would happen under his watch.

Despite breaking his word to supposedly reduce costs, transport fees *still rose* by 4.2%.[3] This came as a direct contradiction to another one of Johnson's original manifesto promises: that he would reduce transport fees over his tenure as mayor.[4] Instead, they rose faster than inflation.

LYING ABOUT SUPPORT FOR THE UNHOUSED

Johnson also broke his promise on rough sleeping in the capital. In 2009, he pledged to end it in London by 2012.[1] Not only did Johnson fail to deliver, but rough sleeping actually doubled over the course of his mayoralty.[2] This increase exceeded the national average.

LYING ABOUT SUPPORT FOR VICTIMS OF SEXUAL VIOLENCE

Johnson's worst broken promise concerned the funding of rape crisis centres. In his election campaign he promised to increase funding to £744,000 a year, enough to fund the existing centre and three more.[1] Less than a year after becoming mayor, Johnson back-tracked on this promise and committed less than half of the promised amount.[2]

Johnson's lack of shame about any of this has had stark consequences for the most vulnerable in our society. Behind each of these broken commitments lie victims who have lost their jobs, can't access vital services, or are unhoused. When you look at the repeated pattern of Johnson's lies, it seems clear he never cared about any of these causes anyway, instead exploiting the powerless in his endless pursuit of power.

LYING ABOUT HIS OWN RECORD AS MAYOR

The lies about his mayoralty didn't end with his mayoralty. Years after leaving office, Johnson still continues to lie and fabricate statistics to try to make his underwhelming time as Mayor of London seem more impressive.

During a special edition of the BBC's *Question Time* in the run up to the 2019 General Election, Johnson claimed he had "massively outbuilt Labour" in housing during his time as mayor.[1] This is, wait for it, a lie. Boris's City Hall presided over an average of 26,144 houses built a year, less than Livingstone's 26,474 or Khan's 35,747.[2] He can claim to have built more affordable housing than his predecessor largely because he changed the definition of affordable housing in 2011[3] to make it *less affordable*.

LYING ABOUT STOP AND SEARCH

He has repeatedly lied about the effectiveness of his "stop and search" policies in London, proven to be racially discriminatory.[1] He claimed to have taken 11,000 knives off the streets using stop and search, but this number totals all knives confiscated by any means in London, with the number for stop and searches alone being estimated at less than half of that number *at most*.[2] He also claimed the policy was responsible for a drop in knife crime,[3] which is directly refuted by a Home Office report looking at the impacts of the policy.[4]

He also claimed to have "cut the murder rate by 50%" as mayor despite it only falling from 155 in 2008 to 109 in 2016.[5] That was either a lie or he is terrible at maths. As if to outdo himself, he also claimed he had cut the murder rate to under 100 for five years in a row when in actual fact the annual number only went below 100 *once* in his eight years as mayor.[6]

Boris even lied about his bike being stolen. As supposed proof of how crime ridden London had become after he left the mayoralty, Johnson claimed that his bike, having never been stolen while he was mayor, had been "nicked" in 2019 under Sadiq Khan.[7] But Johnson was caught out in his lies by a previous article he had written in 2014, claiming the same bike, nicknamed "Bikey", had been destroyed by the weather.[8] A lie of this nature is so trivial it could lead one to reasonably conclude his lying is pathological, and we haven't even gotten to Brexit yet.

BORIS THE LYING BREXITEER

—

LYING ABOUT "BENDY BANANAS"

You've probably heard this one repeated by Johnson and his disciples more than once. In 2016, while beginning his pro-Brexit campaign tour of the country on his big red battle bus (itself emblazoned with another stone-faced lie, which we will get to later), Boris Johnson said it was "absolutely crazy" that the EU dictated how bendy our bananas could be.[1]

Unlike lots of Johnson's lies, this is one he didn't make up all by himself. The myth actually dates back to 1994 – when a "journalist" for the *Sun* published an article claiming that European bureaucrats had just outlawed "curved bananas".[2]

So, is there any truth to it? Obviously not – has this book taught you nothing yet? This myth is loosely based on a piece of regulation from 1994 aiming to make sure bananas met consumer expectations and could be classified by quality for international trade.[3] The law doesn't ban bendy bananas – it says that bananas with "defects of shape" are in the lowest class of bananas but can still be sold.[4] To add just a touch more nonsense, the law wasn't dreamed up by disconnected EU bureaucrats but specifically requested by an interest group made up of European farmers,[5] people who might know a thing or two about what shape a banana should be.

Instead of being an overbearing piece of pointless bureaucracy, the so-called "bendy bananas law" existed to stop consumers from buying produce that wasn't fit for consumption. If only there was a similar law for our politicians.

LYING ABOUT THE EUROPEAN UNION

The shape of bananas is only the tip of the iceberg when it comes to lies Johnson has fabricated about the EU. There isn't time to list every single lie but here are a few of the worst he told during the 2016 referendum campaign.

LYING ABOUT LORRY SAFETY

Johnson blamed the EU for stopping the UK from making lorries safer.[1] In actual fact, the European Parliament voted for legislation to make lorries safer in 2014, legislation which was initially opposed by the UK government. To make matters worse, Boris himself is quoted as being "deeply concerned" by the UK's lack of support for the legislation.[2]

LYING ABOUT CHILDREN BLOWING UP BALLOONS

While on the campaign trail, Johnson claimed that the EU bans children from blowing up balloons. Of course, no such law exists. This was just hot air. In reality, the EU had issued warnings for children under the age of eight to be supervised after several children died blowing them up. This lie is particularly significant, as Johnson coughed it up as his first example of an EU rule he would scrap. Allowing children to die blowing up balloons seems a noble freedom for which to give up visa-free travel, access to the world's largest free market, and stable peace in Ireland.[1]

LYING ABOUT THE EURO

Boris also lied about our obligations to the Eurozone, saying the UK could be forced to bail it out were it to fail. In actual fact, the UK had an agreement with the EU which ensured that, should the budget be used to bail out the Euro, the UK would be "immediately and fully compensated".[1]

LYING ABOUT TRAINS

Finally, Boris told the *Andrew Marr Show* that the EU demanded Crossrail tunnels were 50% bigger to allow German trains to fit through them. In fact, the Crossrail project received a special and specific exemption from the Directive Johnson was referring to.[1] It was just a complete and total lie.

Taken individually, perhaps these lies might seem relatively harmless mistruths, but when taken together, they falsely paint the picture of an overbearing and dangerous European Union that is completely removed from reality. Johnson had been telling these kinds of lies since the beginning of his career as a journalist. As a result, this fictitious version of the EU bled into the public consciousness and framed people's views of it, forever changing the course of history.

LYING ABOUT THE NHS ON THE SIDE OF A BUS

This lie is maybe Johnson's most infamous to date and could probably be singled out as the one that has most deeply impacted your life. It is, of course, the claim that the UK sent £350 million a week to the EU which could be spent on the NHS, emblazoned across the side of Vote Leave's battle bus.

This lie was repeated time and time again by the Vote Leave campaign generally and Boris Johnson in particular. This lie was so brazen it led the independent UK Statistics Authority to criticise Johnson for "a clear misuse of official statistics".[1] This figure does not take into account the massive rebate the UK received from the EU, nor any money it received back from the EU for subsidies or funding for programmes [2], which amount to tens of millions of pounds.

A study in 2018 found that a shocking 42% of the public still believed the UK sent that much money to the EU.[3] Dominic Cummings, the chief Vote Leave strategist and master of deception in his own right, admitted that without the claim Vote Leave likely would have lost the referendum.[4] Johnson effectively defrauded the public by lying to them in order to win the referendum.

LYING ABOUT TURKEY'S FUTURE MEMBERSHIP OF THE EU

Throughout the referendum campaign, the Vote Leave campaign repeatedly lied about Turkey's supposed impending membership of the European Union. Of course, Johnson was no exception to this.

Immigration was among the top two reasons people voted to leave the European Union [1], related in part to the lie that Turkey would join the EU and a large influx of Turkish migrants would come to the UK. Indeed, a poll showed 67% of the British public opposed Turkey joining.[2]

Johnson played into these fears, claiming that the UK population would rise "inexorably" if we stayed in the EU.[3] He also co-signed a letter claiming the only way to stop a shared border with Turkey was to vote leave.[4] None of this was true. Although Turkey had applied to join the EU, there was no question of it joining imminently, and doing so would require the UK to explicitly agree to it, so it would be impossible for Turkey to join against our will.[5] We had quite a bit of control *in* the European Union. This lie was designed to play on people's immigration fears and align with Nigel Farage's xenophobic "breaking point" arguments.[6]

Boris must have known this lie was wrong (or just have a terrible memory) as he has since lied about having ever talked about Turkey at all during the referendum campaign.[7] Apart from the letter he co-signed and the countless times he mentioned Turkey in interviews (of which videos exist).[8] Johnson was, of course, on the Vote Leave campaign committee, which created numerous posters and ads based on the claim that Turkey was about to join the EU.[9] As always with him, there is nothing he won't try and lie his way out of.

BY KYLE TAYLOR

MIDDLE NOTE: A POLITICS FOREVER CHANGED

When Boris Johnson began his rise to power you wouldn't have been alone if you thought of the entire thing as a bit of a laugh. The floppy hair, the foppish nature, the cheeky grin. He seemed different. Not politics as usual. A breath of fresh air even. What sat just beneath the surface, however, was the most political, most ruthless, and most self-serving politician in modern British history.

Boris Johnson isn't alone in this. He's part of a global cohort of narcissistic egomaniacs who will say and do anything for power and then say or do anything to hang onto it, even if it means becoming completely detached from truth. In fact, it requires it because the most effective way to build and maintain support in politics is to become the arbiter of truth yourself or to simply create so much uncertainty around truth that people simply don't know what to believe.

For those who have followed the saga of Boris Johnson closely it's easy to wonder how he continued to rise when it was overwhelmingly obvious that he was a compulsively lying charlatan. The bed of nails principle helps to explain it. You may have seen a performer lie on a bed of nails before. It seems impossible but because the weight of the person is distributed over so many nails, there's not enough pressure on any one individual nail to break the skin. It's the same in politics. If there are tons and tons of scandals, lies, and half-truths, each one a metaphorical nail, none breaks the skin so the politician survives, as

Boris did for so long and as Trump did for so long as well. Meanwhile, if there's just one nail, like Hillary Clinton's fake email scandal, it goes right through.

The impact of this, however, extends far beyond Boris Johnson's own survival. It rewires our politics. We stop being sure of what is true and what isn't. With so much uncertainty, we look to the individuals on our "side" to help us make sense of the world. Over time, that shared reality that binds society together – the facts from which we all operate – disappear and we suddenly find ourselves living in different truths and different worlds, unable to function as a society any more. We're leavers or remainers. We're "woke" or we're "anti-cancel culture". Bill Gates nanobotters or anti-vaxxers. No matter the issue, there are two tribes and we must be in one. We spend endless hours on social media attacking the "other" and commiserating with "our people" who know "the truth".

It often feels like there is no way back and that is the real effect of the self-serving politician. He doesn't care, as long as it keeps him in power. Boris Johnson's impact on our politics, our culture, and our country is only just beginning to be felt. The long shadow of his degradation of public life and of truth itself will be his legacy. Indeed, it *must* be his legacy. He doesn't deserve to write history any more. It's our turn now.

PART 2

BORIS THE LYING
PRIME MINISTER

ELECTION LIES, IMAGINARY ACCOMPLISHMENTS, AND COVID-19

—

LYING ABOUT HIS REASONS FOR SEEKING OFFICE

Johnson claimed on numerous occasions that he never wanted to be Prime Minister in the first place.[1] In 2019, he insisted that he had no choice but to call a snap general election because MPs wouldn't back his rushed Brexit deal. This came after Parliament rejected his plans to "Get Brexit Done", accusing him of avoiding proper scrutiny by accelerating the timetable.[2] He genuinely sought to convince us that he had no ambitions for power, and that he cared so much about Britain that he simply *needed* to be PM to help us escape the terrifying clutches of the European Union – on his own specific terms, of course. The irony is that he withdrew the Brexit Bill himself[3] to create the scenario he then used to justify the election.

It's hard to deny that he was only in office to enrich himself and his cronies while inflating his own ego. Are we truly supposed to believe that the man who avoided accountability at every turn, spent undisclosed Tory donor money furnishing the publicly owned Prime Minister's flat [4], and had a great deal of fun appointing his donors and mates to the House of Lords for life [5] truly sought the role of PM out of a sense of *responsibility*?

Consider the simple story of Johnson having written two op-eds for the *Telegraph*, one advocating for Brexit and one making the case for remain, both drafted shortly before his personal brand-launch as a Brexiteer when just one was published.[6] This supposed champion of the people was quite literally deciding which side to take based on which one he thought would further his career – not which one he actually believed in.

Those around him knew this well. David Cameron famously called him out for not believing in Brexit and simply hopping on the bandwagon.[7] Ideally, most people would agree that an elected representative should actually care about things.

LYING ABOUT HIS ACCOMPLISHMENTS (AGAIN)

Boris Johnson has imagined so many fake accomplishments that this book would be biblical in length if we were to try to catalogue all of them individually. A common scene during Prime Minister's Questions would consist of Opposition MPs decrying whatever scandal Johnson was embroiled in that week and Johnson responding by rattling off a nonsensical list of his administration's supposed achievements. To his credit, he reached levels of bravado and bluster during these absurd moments never seen before.

This is just the tip of the iceberg when it comes to Boris Johnson's highly honed art of deflection, gaslighting, and misrepresentation. It's a serious problem when you can't even ask the PM a simple question because he'll start spouting unrelated lies about how successful he's been. The scariest part about this strategy is that – for a time at least – it worked. It's unnerving to think about how long Johnson evaded scrutiny by simply deflecting with made-up achievements. The lies did catch up to him in the end, though it seems there are still people hanging on to every word of his deceptive gloating, and conveniently ignoring reality. Here's a sampling of the misleading and false claims he's made about his record in government.

LYING ABOUT THE ECONOMY

One of Johnson's favourite retorts to criticism in Parliament was the declaration that he had created the "fastest growing economy in the G7". His aim was to pretend his government was managing the economy so well, we were actually outperforming the other advanced economies in the G7: France, Canada, the USA, Japan, Germany, and Italy (and that this was all down to him). Unfortunately, he was warping the statistics, and comparing one narrow period of relative growth when more conventional analysis would have placed the UK in fifth place.[1] Moreover, he neglected to mention that our economy had shrunk a ridiculous 21% in 2020 (the worst recession since 1709), giving the UK significantly more room to bounce back than the competitors he mentioned because their economies hadn't fallen nearly as far.[2] He's also claimed that the UK had the lowest corporate tax rate in Europe during a TV debate (it doesn't) [3], and that his government had grown the UK economy by 73%, a ludicrously large number for any government in such a short period of time for which Dawn Butler MP (a co-author of this book) famously called him out.[4]

LYING ABOUT POVERTY

Johnson has also made a number of proclamations attempting to rebrand his abysmal record on poverty. In 2020, he claimed that under his government, both relative and absolute poverty had declined. In reality, relative poverty has not fallen but generally *risen* over the last decade, including under his administration, and while absolute poverty declined slightly under

Theresa May's government, that was not the case once he took over. He went on to say that 400,000 fewer families were living in poverty in 2020 than in 2010, a figure which he completely made up.[1] It's no surprise that a government (and political party) with records on poverty like Johnson's feel compelled to invent numbers that suit them.

LYING ABOUT CRIME

In response to the publication of the Sue Gray report, which detailed Johnson's reckless and illegal partying during COVID-19 lockdowns (as will be discussed further along in this book), Johnson boasted about his government's supposed accomplishments on crime. Unfortunately they were imaginary, claiming that he brought down crime by 14%. This was actually a reversal of the statistics in the report from the Office for National Statistics, which showed that crime had *risen* by 14% [1]!

LYING ABOUT COVID-19 TEST AND TRACE

Johnson boldly proclaimed during the COVID-riddled summer of 2020 that no country on Earth had a functioning test and trace app. This claim, of course, came immediately after it was revealed that the government-funded and custom-tailored

COVID-tracking app would be abandoned and left to the private sector, squandering the millions of pounds of taxpayers' money already spent. His remarks were likely quite insulting to Germany and other nations that had already developed functional apps.[1]

LYING ABOUT CLIMATE VICTORIES

As we saw with COVID, Johnson loves to take credit for handling a crisis while doing basically nothing. He claimed at the 2021 climate change summit COP26 that the UK was a "world leader" on climate, "far ahead of the pack", insinuating that his valiant leadership magically made the UK more sustainable.[1] Funny then that he'd dodge a major climate change debate with party leaders [2] and feel the need to lie about his role in the development of nuclear fusion energy generation technologies that *literally do not exist.*[3]

LYING ABOUT GETTING "THE BIG CALLS RIGHT"

In his final speech to Parliament, Boris repeated another favourite boast of his. With an implicit *although I've been horrendously corrupt*, Boris claimed after his resignation (and not for the first time) that he still "got all the big calls right".[1] In reality, though, he bungled just about everything he touched. As this book illustrates, he utterly failed on COVID,

Brexit, Ukraine, managing the economy, protecting democracy, and more.[2] He'll be remembered as a leader you couldn't trust as far as you could throw him; someone truly out only for himself.

LYING ABOUT "GETTING BREXIT DONE"

The final example too obvious not to bring up here is Johnson's constant boasting about how his government managed to "get Brexit done" – going back all the way to the campaign trail.[1] Sure, he technically saw us out of the European Union. Something about the bragging, though, seems to imply that any of it actually delivered on the promises he made. Moreover, it doesn't seem truly done, as the government continues to threaten to withdraw from parts of the agreement designed to maintain peace in Ireland, with Boris specifically seeking to portray himself as a victim of the Northern Ireland protocol *he agreed to*.[2]

LYING TO THE QUEEN ABOUT PROROGATION

Yes, even the late Queen Elizabeth II herself is on the long list of people Boris Johnson is accused of deliberately misleading. In August 2019, the Queen prorogued Parliament upon Johnson's request, conveniently sending Parliamentarians home for a five-week period right before the UK's scheduled exit from the European Union. Johnson had told the Queen that he simply wanted to redefine his policy agenda with a new Queen's Speech.[1]

Scottish judges unanimously ruled that Boris Johnson had misled the Queen and acted in bad faith by giving Her Majesty false advice. They claimed that his real intention had been to impede the Opposition's ability to analyse his Brexit plans.[2] The UK Supreme Court ultimately ruled that the prorogation was "unlawful", imposing unjustified executive authority and undermining Parliament. It ruled the prorogation as void.[3] The whole fiasco demonstrated the extreme lengths to which Johnson was willing to go in order to avoid democratic scrutiny of his hastily concocted Brexit plans.

Unsurprisingly, Johnson denied lying to the Queen and reiterated his supposed reasons for suspending Parliament.[4] When the Supreme Court ruling came out, he was forced to cut short his trip to New York, arriving home to proclaim that he "strongly disagreed" with the court and that he wouldn't rule out making another attempt to suspend Parliament.[5] Uncoincidentally, Boris would later introduce legislation to undermine democratic accountability by making it significantly harder to challenge the government in the courts. It would seem he is capable of learning from his mistakes, but only in the worst, most authoritarian way.[6]

LYING ABOUT HIS COVID-19 RESPONSE

Johnson has generally taken credit for tackling the COVID-19 pandemic, emphasising his phenomenal vaccine rollout and how seriously he's taken the crisis. The reality looked quite different: Johnson missing the first COBRA meetings about COVID (which were already held quite late into the pandemic), engaging in contract cronyism, rolling out the infection travesty that was Eat Out to Help Out, and generally prioritising the economy over mitigating the virus, and that's all before we even get to Partygate.[1]

Johnson gaslit the public at a truly unprecedented level. He wanted to be perceived as a Churchill-esque figure, staring down a major crisis with bravery and a willingness to make the tough calls. So much for the man who supposedly never wanted to be Prime Minister. Of course, it's hard to lead an anxious nation through an international catastrophe when your first priority is yourself.

His self-styled commitment to the public was undercut when it was discovered he was being directly advised by an anti-lockdown scientist bankrolled by billionaire Tory donors.[2] This contributed to the "herd immunity" strategies condemned by public health experts.[3] It was an excuse to prioritise the wants of his billionaire donors over the public health needs of the public, lying to the public by suggesting that herd immunity could be created through high levels of infection (which would of course mean more deaths) when such a strategy requires high levels of vaccination.[4] It certainly didn't help when his ministers created a "VIP lane" for COVID-related contracts, leading to faulty masks and unusable PPE while enriching many of the PM's mates.[5]

The UK had the most deaths per capita of all G7 nations during the first two major waves of the pandemic.[5] Even when you leave out the obvious fiasco that was Partygate (don't worry, we *will* get to it), Johnson's leadership through the pandemic was an abject failure that cost the lives of over 200,000 people.[6] The government did indeed "let the bodies pile high" [7], as Johnson is alleged to have said.

LYING ABOUT THE VACCINE ROLLOUT

Boris Johnson claimed multiple times that the UK was successful in dealing with COVID-19 because of the "freedoms" granted by Brexit. He claimed that the UK had the fastest vaccine and booster rollouts due to the liberties afforded it by leaving the EU.[1]

The implication was that the EU put a burden on the regulatory process with its so-called "overbearing" regulations, and now the UK was free to develop vital medicines faster. Unfortunately for Boris (and the rest of us), the UK's rollout was only the fastest in Europe for a brief period and was overtaken by a number of other countries after the vaccination rate plateaued in 2021.[1] As of June 2022, the UK had a vaccination rate of 73%, placing it 16th in Europe.[2]

Furthermore, the vaccine was administered and authorised under EU law – because the UK was still in the Brexit transitional period at the time and had used emergency powers to distribute a vaccine. The head of the MHRA confirmed this on live television shortly after Johnson, Matt Hancock, and Jacob Rees-Mogg all misrepresented the truth on Twitter and in Parliament.[3]

"GLOBAL BRITAIN": FOREIGN POLICY AND MORE BREXIT

—

LYING ABOUT REFUGEES AND ASYLUM SEEKERS

Johnson would have us believe that the UK is "out in front" of the pack when it comes to looking after refugees.[1] At one Prime Minister's Questions, Johnson's government was accused of failing to support Ukrainian refugees in the wake of Putin's invasion of their country in February 2022. He responded by claiming that the UK has "done more to resettle vulnerable people than any other European government since 2015". This only refers to resettlement schemes, which are a small part of the larger asylum system. By established metrics, the UK is behind Germany, France, Sweden, Italy, and Spain in terms of accepting refugees. When you consider the number of people accepted as a proportion of population, the UK comes 20th in Europe.[2]

This lie speaks to something a bit darker, however: Johnson sought to paint the UK as an inviting beacon of liberty when it's abundantly clear that this nation is not always a welcoming one. Johnson not only failed to invite in as many Ukrainian refugees as other countries, but also failed at taking care of those that did arrive. According to some estimates, 50,000 Ukrainian refugees could be made homeless by 2023.[3] The Homes for Ukraine scheme designed to house migrants began falling apart in the summer of 2022 and Boris took no action to offer renewed support.[3]

While we're considering Johnson's insinuation that the UK is a bastion of freedom for refugees and asylum seekers, let's also remember the migrants coming from other parts of the world. Johnson's Nationality and Borders Act criminalises asylum seekers, erodes protections against human trafficking, and gives the Home Office powers to deport asylum seekers to other countries. Indeed, we saw it in practice when then Home Secretary Priti Patel tried to deport asylum seekers to Rwanda.[4] She failed to do so, thanks to the lawyers that Boris Johnson condemned as radical left-wing "legal eagles".[5]

LYING ABOUT FOREIGN INTERFERENCE IN ELECTIONS

In 2019, not too long after taking office and illegally proroguing Parliament, Boris Johnson assured the public that there was "no evidence" of Russian interference in UK elections.[1] He insisted that he wasn't sure how much money was donated to his party by Russian nationals, but that donations were surely registered appropriately. Perhaps unsurprisingly, a March 2019 report by Parliament's Intelligence and Security Committee (ISC) investigating potential Russian interference in the Brexit referendum was blocked from publication at Johnson's order.[1]

Johnson dismissed the accusations as "Bermuda triangle stuff", while his party *almost simultaneously* accepted a £200,000 donation from the wife of a former Russian government official. In a desperate attempt to keep the report away from public scrutiny, Johnson sought to appoint a loyal ally MP as head of the Committee, which its members rejected.[2] Ultimately, the report came out heavily redacted. Sources near the ISC confirmed the redaction of specific names went far beyond Downing Street's authority. Johnson worked hard to censor evidence-driven debate about interference and likely lied about the lack of evidence.[3]

While incredibly conspicuous, the cover-up attempts felt nothing short of desperate. Boris also appointed Evgeny Lebedev, the son of a former Soviet spy who once operated in London, to a lifetime appointment in the UK House of Lords as – wait for it – Baron Lebedev of Hampton in the London Borough of Richmond upon Thames *and of Siberia in the Russian Federation*.[4]

LYING ABOUT NORTHERN IRELAND AND BREXIT

"There will be no border in the Irish Sea… over my dead body." Those are the lying words of a certain Alexander Boris de Pfeffel Johnson, speaking to the *Irish News* in 2020.[1] In the original Brexit withdrawal agreement, the Northern Ireland Protocol was agreed between the UK and the EU as a means to keep trade moving between the Republic of Ireland (in the EU) and Northern Ireland (in the UK). It was also deeply political due to the tense history in the area. The primary reason the EU and the UK agreed the protocol was to maintain the Good Friday Agreement.[2] Johnson had promised there would be "no checks on goods going from GB to NI, or NI to GB"[3] in an attempt to show that Brexit would be successful under his withdrawal agreement.

Then he hit us with a classic Johnson U-turn of epic proportions – a lie to undo a lie. The Northern Ireland Protocol Bill, introduced in 2022 and still working its way through Parliament at the time of writing, explicitly removes the border in the Irish Sea, likely forcing a hard border in Ireland, which is the only way the European Union can reasonably maintain its single market. This immediately undermines the Good Friday Agreement and peace in Ireland that Johnson's government claimed to defend. The government has admitted that the bill will renege on their promises under international law, but claims legality over a "doctrine of necessity" – a power to make amendments to the agreement under extreme conditions, which were not present at the time of signing.[4] MEPs in the European Parliament have called the bill "a serious breach of international law" that calls into question the UK's general credibility.[5]

The most amazing part of this whole debacle is the extreme gaslighting Boris Johnson and his ministers deployed. Their entire argument was predicated on the idea that *their own protocol* was now such a disaster that it necessitated their use of the "doctrine of necessity". Brexit negotiator Lord Frost also claimed that the original protocol was "imposed under duress" because the UK had not left the EU yet and we were not a sovereign nation.[6] Simultaneously, Johnson tried to claim that the bill was nothing but a minor bureaucratic squabble. Their statements are, of course, nonsensical and their actions threaten to unravel the delicate peace arrangements in place in Northern Ireland. Johnson once again showed us that his promises about Brexit were nothing more than a thin veneer of populism around a void of corruption, lies, and deception.

LYING ABOUT THE IMPACT OF BREXIT

As France began treating the UK as a third country in 2020 following the UK's official departure from the European Union, lorries attempting to get to the EU immediately clogged the M20 in Kent.[1] Johnson popped up to issue some lies in an attempt to smooth over the controversy. Praising his own "long-term plans" for Brexit, he claimed that he had reduced the number of lorries from 500 to 170. The time-frame he referred to was not at all clear. Reporters instantly closed in to say that all official sources, including Kent council's highways department, maintained that there were still easily 500 lorries on the M20. Later that day, official numbers reached nearly 1,000. Video footage emerged that disproved the claims, yet Downing Street refused to issue a correction.[1]

This lie is symbolic of the attitude of Johnson's government when engaging with the catastrophic fallout of Brexit. While Johnson has long attempted to conflate the negative impact on markets, trade, finance, and more with the COVID-19 pandemic, experts have been able to isolate Brexit's costs at roughly £100 billion a year in lost output.[2] This is coupled with the chronic labour shortages due to declining numbers of European workers in the country and failure to achieve the higher wages that Brexit was promised to provide.[3] Additionally, the lack of self-determination is tangible, especially given that now a majority of the country seems to think Brexit was a mistake.[4]

So what was Boris Johnson's approach to the failure of his defining issue? Lying. It's lying. One early distraction was the promise that we'd secure a better trading deal with the United States, which never materialised.[5] Aside from blaming the pandemic for our dire economic straits, he's also gotten a number of jabs in at the EU bureaucrats for supposedly making the situation worse, despite the fact that we supposedly took back control. How could EU bureaucrats still be causing problems?

His scapegoating of "EU Red Tape" manifested in the Brexit Freedoms Bill which removes all kinds of environmental and labour protections on businesses in order to ostensibly *give us more freedom* and make sure the public blames the EU instead of his rotten leadership.[6] The promise of Brexit, it seems, remains somewhere over the horizon, never to be reached because it doesn't actually exist.

LYING ABOUT THE EUROPEAN CONVENTION ON HUMAN RIGHTS

In 2016, Johnson described the European Convention on Human Rights (ECHR) as "one of the great things we gave to Europe".[1] The ECHR was set up in the 1950s, following the horrors of the Second World War, pioneered by none other than Winston Churchill. It expanded on the UN's Human Rights Declaration, and led to the creation of the European Court of Human Rights (ECHR), which is charged with enforcing the convention, which obliges nations to protect and respect the inherent rights of citizens.[2]

The UK's Human Rights Act (HRA) was brought into force later on in 1998, to help UK citizens access justice under the ECHR standards.[3]

Unsurprisingly, Boris's pride regarding his hero's role in creating this system evaporated the second the rights it guaranteed became a challenge to his draconian policies. Once judges stopped him from deporting refugees to Rwanda, he almost immediately began discussing serious plans for withdrawing the UK from its jurisdiction.[4] His plan, halted temporarily by his successor Liz Truss, had been to instead create a new British Bill of Rights outside of the European Convention.

The Law Society has said that the impacts of the new Bill of Rights would be devastating. They'd make it nigh impossible to challenge deportations regardless of the legitimacy of the claim, add barriers to accessing justice, remove the courts' duty to follow ECHR principles, and restrict public bodies from owing "positive obligations" (essentially meaning they can't take proactive measures to protect people's rights).[4]

Nothing is sacred to Johnson except himself. Not even his role model Winston Churchill.

PERSONAL CONDUCT, POLITICAL SMEARS, AND SCANDALS

—

LYING ABOUT HIS OWN CONDUCT

Johnson has said some truly delusional things about himself and the way that he operates. It's unclear whether it's an image he's knowingly striving to create, or whether he actually believes these things to be true.

In an ITV news interview in 2019, Johnson was asked if he had ever lied during his political career. "Absolutely not," he responded.[1] Johnson claims that he's never once tried to deceive the public. He then qualified his remarks by adding that it's possible he's made a mistake once or twice. It is possible that he doesn't actually think he is lying?

Last year, he hit us with another uniquely Orwellian soundbite at COP26, claiming that "those who break the rules must be investigated and should be punished".[2] This is the exact same man who, not long after, went on to change Parliament's Ministerial Code solely to save his own skin.[3] This year, asked if he would take responsibility for the Tories' local election defeats in May, he delivered another belter: "I always take responsibility for everything." [4]

LYING ABOUT POLITICAL SMEARS

Listing all of the political smears Boris Johnson has used to disparage political opponents would require its own volume. Projecting insults seems as natural to Johnson as breathing. He follows the classic pattern of accusing his opponents of the very same things he's done himself. It's a textbook authoritarian tactic. Below are just a few.

The Labour Party is generally the focal point of Johnson's baseless attacks. He claimed during an interview in 2019 that Labour wanted to disband MI5 and abandon NATO.[1] These were both untrue accusations that did not reflect the party's official platform, though Jeremy Corbyn had been critical of NATO in the past.[1] He worked hard to paint a picture of Corbyn as a Russian agent, referring to him as "Vladimir Corbyn" during Prime Minister's Questions and insinuating that Keir Starmer was involved too because he campaigned for Corbyn.[2]

It's difficult to think Boris wasn't projecting here, given his connections with Russian officials and money.[3]

Boris has also called out Keir Starmer for voting "48 times" to "undo the will of the people", referring to Brexit. This is unequivocally false, and referred to 48 votes related to anything remotely to do with the European Union instead of on the matter itself.[4]

Then came Beergate. Referring to Starmer as "Sir Beer Korma", Johnson proclaimed that Starmer had no room to talk about his own partying during lockdowns because the Labour leader had done the same thing. He referred, of course, to a photograph of Starmer having a beer with staff after an election-related campaigning meeting when some non-work restrictions remained.[5] Calling Johnson's bluff, Starmer agreed to resign if he was given a police fine, challenging Boris to do the same.[6] He didn't, of course.

Ultimately, Starmer was cleared in the probe of his conduct during lockdown.[6] Johnson was not, but we'll come to that in a moment. Not unlike his bragging, With Boris, when the accusations start flying, he starts lying.

LYING ABOUT ALMOST EVERYTHING

Buckle up, reader. You're about to get deeply, deeply angry as this section outlines the lies Johnson has told over the years in defence of the indefensible. His administration was one plagued with scandal, and it wasn't limited merely to his own conduct. It's time to lay out just a few of the biggest scandals and the lies Johnson told about them.

Dominic Cummings: In 2020, when Cummings was Chief Adviser to Boris Johnson, he was enveloped in scandal for breaking his own government's lockdown rules (a theme). Johnson vigorously defended Cummings, claiming that he acted "responsibly and with integrity".[1] Johnson claimed to have seen evidence that would acquit Cummings, but Number 10 refused to publish it. Durham Constabulary ultimately ruled it a minor breach due to lack of evidence and didn't pursue the matter further.[2] It was apparently totally reasonable to test your eyesight by driving 25 miles to a castle.[3]

Matt Hancock: In 2021, Johnson's Health Secretary Matt Hancock was pictured kissing his aide in violation of social distancing rules. Matt Hancock resigned shortly thereafter, with Boris emphasising that he was not pressured to quit. Afterwards, he claimed that Hancock's resignation was the right thing and that Hancock was undermining the government's message of facing the pandemic all together.[4] Earlier in 2021, a high court ruled that Hancock's department had acted unlawfully by failing to publish COVID PPE contracts on time. Boris Johnson was accused of misleading Parliament when he said they were "on record for everyone to see". The Cabinet Secretary cleared the PM for this move, but a cross-party group of MPs voiced vocal opposition to this decision.[5] A later ruling would determine that Hancock's use of a "VIP lane" for those contracts was illegal. That just might explain their unwillingness to publish the contracts at the time.[6]

Priti Patel: In 2020, the Home Secretary was famously accused of treating her staff with disrespect and abuse. An official investigation by an independent adviser described it as "bullying". Johnson immediately rushed to her defence, attempting to convince the adviser, Sir Alex Allan, to tone down findings in the report. Johnson ultimately overruled Sir Alex's conclusions, protecting Patel from reprimand under the Ministerial Code.[7]

Owen Paterson: In 2021, former cabinet minister Owen Paterson was alleged to have egregiously broken lobbying rules. Johnson attempted to protect him by replacing Parliament's disciplinary system abruptly with a Tory-led Committee, rushed through in a last-minute vote. He then attempted to claim that he thought there would be cross-party support for the overhaul – a laughable idea.[8]

Of course, there's far more that could be discussed here. What's clear is that Johnson appoints equally contemptible people, lies at every turn, and obstructs justice. His narcissism and sense of invincibility would never allow for ministerial resignations, so he chose instead to lie to the faces of his colleagues and the country.

LYING ABOUT PARTYING, THEN LYING ABOUT PARTYGATE

This is the big one. There's a fairly large number of lies associated with Partygate. This scandal was symbolic in a significant way – it showed that Johnson truly viewed himself as completely untouchable. He clearly didn't care about the devastating impact his failed leadership had on the lives of people across the country. He continued with this lie until the evidence *should have been* insurmountable. Here's a timeline of Johnson's denials:

December 1st, 2021: Johnson defended himself against Keir Starmer's accusations of inappropriate behaviour at Prime Minister's Questions, claiming that "all guidance was completely followed". He accused Starmer of "playing politics", whining about wallpaper and parties [1] .

December 3rd, 2021: On a visit to a vaccine centre, Johnson claimed multiple times that "we followed the guidance at all times". Even when pressed on it, he persisted.[1]

December 7th, 2021: Boris claimed yet again that "all the guidance was observed".[1] Leaked footage of Allegra Stratton, then Downing Street Press Secretary, shows government officials joking about having a party. Johnson still insists that "there was no Christmas party".[2]

December 8th, 2021: Johnson claimed that the video made him "sickened and furious", but gave assurances that still no wrongdoing took place. In addition, he separately denied another charge about a party on November 13th.[1]

December 13th, 2021: Boris said, "I certainly broke no rules." [1]

December 20th, 2021: Johnson defended himself after photos emerged of another garden party at Downing Street. Boris assured the public that "those were people at work, talking about work" – despite the wine, cheese, and numerous people standing in different parts of the garden.[1]

The public were ultimately left waiting for the publication of the Sue Gray report, which was set to outline the extent of wrongdoing on the part of the PM and his colleagues. Johnson was accused of pressing Sue Gray to "dilute" the report by omitting names and leaving out key events.[3] Ultimately, it did come out, and the findings were shocking. Gray described *fifteen* parties, eight of which were attended by Boris Johnson. She describes extreme rowdiness, puking from drinking too much, and even what sounded like a minor fist-fight. Lockdown rules were indeed broken, and she described the events as "failures of leadership and judgement in No 10 and the Cabinet Office".[4] This also meant that Boris Johnson had repeatedly, and blatantly, lied to the public about his actions, in addition to disrespecting the hundreds of thousands of families bereaved by COVID-19.

Sue Gray's report noted that security and custodial staff were mocked for warning about COVID-19 guidelines, and treated with "disrespect".[5] In one particularly tragic story, a custodial staff member at the Ministry of Justice, Emanuel Gomes, suffered abuse from the PM's staff during the lockdown parties. Gomes later passed away from COVID-19 in 2020, after the reported parties.[5]

LYING ABOUT PROMOTING A SEX PEST – THE ONE THAT GOT HIM IN THE END

Something had to bring Boris down eventually. He really did make it through a lot of lying before it all came crashing down on him. The Chris Pincher scandal was the last nail in the coffin. It's what brought in the letters of no-confidence that ultimately led to Johnson's resignation. Of course, the whole story was also riddled with lies from the PM.

Chris Pincher, a Conservative MP, resigned as Deputy Chief Whip in June 2021 following allegations that he'd groped two men at a club in central London. Boris hesitated to suspend him from the party, but eventually did so. Questions then emerged over whether the PM knew about Pincher's conduct when he'd appointed him in the first place. Throughout the month of July, the PM's story just kept changing. First, Johnson claimed that he was "not aware of any specific allegations". Then, he claimed he was possibly aware of "media reports" about Pincher's behaviour in the past. Finally, he admitted that he had been informed about a complaint made against Pincher back in 2019.[1] Johnson also failed to deny that he not only knew about it but had nicknamed him "Pincher by name, pincher by nature".[2]

Boris would express his regret, saying that "in hindsight", it was a bad move to appoint a knowingly alleged sexual predator. He claimed that there was "no place in this government for anybody who is a predator or who abuses their position of power". Finally, his usual blustering half-apology strategy wasn't enough. The resignations began piling in almost immediately after that speech, beginning with Health Secretary Sajid Javid.[3] Johnson probably arrogantly thought he was going to slip out of this one, just like every single time before. It's unclear why exactly this was the red line for his Cabinet members. Many of them had stood by him through so much horror that it was somewhat reassuring to know that something could waver their support, though it is deeply troubling that it took so much.

AFTERWORD: A POLITICS FOREVER CHANGED

—

BY PETER STEFANOVIC

I can imagine after reaching the end of this book that you might be asking yourself "How on earth did this man get away with all of this for so long?" You wouldn't be alone, but it brings to life how a seemingly slow trickle of lies and deceit can not only go unnoticed but fundamentally change what we see as normal and acceptable. Indeed, as a lawyer and political commentator I had been focussed on holding power to account for years, and while people were paying attention, it felt for so long that we would never reach critical mass.

That all changed in 2021, when I fact-checked several claims made by Boris Johnson since he had been PM and summarised my findings in a video posted on social media. With the public's incredible support it was watched a staggering 44 million times. Over a period of months it made headlines around the world, exposing archaic parliamentary rules and procedures no longer fit for purpose and a Speaker of the House powerless to act. The film was broadcast and debated on *Good Morning Britain* by Susanna Reid and Alastair Campbell, who championed the film from the start (raising it during interviews on BBC News, Sky News and even *Question Time*). The film played a significant role in educating the public to the fact that Boris Johnson had misled Parliament over and over again – and driven a horse and cart through the Ministerial Code. It was reported as far away as New Zealand and was even projected onto the Houses of Parliament by the brilliant campaigning organisation Led By Donkeys. It prompted the raising of serious questions in Parliament about the Prime Minister's honesty. One Labour MP and a co-author of this book, Dawn Butler, was actually expelled by the Speaker of the House after directly quoting from it and calling the Prime Minister a liar, as she explained to set the scene for this book. It certainly raised a lot of eyebrows in the establishment, and the repercussions of it are still being felt today.

I'm often asked what drove me to take on the political establishment in this way. Quite simply, I could not stand by and allow lying in our politics to become normalised. As lawyers we are supposed to be the advocates. If we don't speak out when our democracy and the rule of law are threatened, who will? Former Tory Prime Minister Sir John Major put it this way:

"In our democracy, we are able to speak truth to power. But, if democracy is to be respected, power must also speak truth to the people."

In our courts the crime of perjury is taken extremely seriously because the very foundation of our legal system depends on trust and credibility. That same principle, to my mind, should apply equally if not more so to our political institutions because if those institutions are undermined by lies and false statements, our very democracy is put at risk. When I think of my late parents I remember, above all else, their unwavering honesty. They would never have lied to or misled anyone and I believe the overwhelming majority of people in this country hold the truth in similarly high regard. Why, then, should we expect less from those holding high office? I simply could not stand by and do nothing.

As lawyers and officers of the Supreme Court I believe we have an absolute duty and responsibility to speak out when the rule of law is threatened. The situation in this country is very grave right now. The Tory government has consistently acted against people and institutions which seek to subject its actions to scrutiny and accountability. You may recall the *Telegraph* reporting that then Attorney General Suella Braverman, now our Home Secretary, had banned lawyers from telling ministers their policies are unlawful! As you've just read, we have witnessed previous Prime Minister Boris Johnson unlawfully prorogue Parliament, rewrite the introduction to the Ministerial Code by tossing out references to the Nolan principles (such as honesty) – and a government willing to break both domestic and international law whenever it suits its own self-interests and political agenda.

As we write, Liz Truss has resigned as Prime Minister and been replaced without a General Election or even a vote of the Conservative Party's own members. She led the country for just 45 days and it was clear that nothing had really changed. We saw yet again a new pattern of misleading statements, U-turns and incompetence that, in a matter of weeks, crashed the pound, sent interest rates skyrocketing, and continued to threaten our basic human rights. These aren't theoretical concepts. We're talking about people's lives. The reality is, the rot at the core of our politics won't stop with the departure of Johnson or Truss.

So how do we stop Prime Ministers who openly mislead Parliament? How do we stop the rot? We know, of course, that it is against the Ministerial Code – the standards of conduct expected of ministers – to lie in Parliament. We also know that ministers who have knowingly broken the Ministerial Code have been expected to resign. Archaic Parliamentary rules, exposed by many of my films, have proved useless and the Speaker has himself admitted he is powerless to act. As Labour MP Dawn Butler said, the difficulty is "the person in charge of determining whether ministers have breached the ministerial code is the chief liar, Boris Johnson himself". It therefore seems to me that the only way forward on this is to wrestle ownership of the Ministerial Code away from the Prime Minister. To my mind – in practical terms – it's the only way to stop those achieving the highest office in the land from openly lying to and misleading Parliament. But that requires a change of government to a party of power that is genuinely committed to cleaning up our politics. That's where you come in.

Yes, vote, of course, but think about what more you can do – knock on doors, march in the streets, speak to family and friends – buy them this book – whatever it takes to ensure that every citizen of this country understands how close we are to the point of no return and how far we must keep people like Boris Johnson and Liz Truss from power. Democracy and our way of life are not a given, nor are they the norm in the course of history. Our institutions, our laws, and our norms must be fought for each and every day and that requires all of us to act. Let's get to work.

ACKNOWLEDGEMENTS

—

This book would not have been possible without our amazing research and drafting team of Matthew Gallagher and Oliver Stanton. Their ability to source absolutely every claim we aimed to make is extraordinary. They kept us on track, on time, and on point. Thank you!

Thanks as well to Ella Baddeley, Stephen Colegrave, and the entire Byline Books team who are building a daring publishing house willing to speak truth to power. Your work inspires us.

To our families and friends who support us, listen to our rants, and remind us to "do something about it", you are the engines that drive us even in those most difficult moments.

Finally, to every person in this country who has had to suffer through the indignity, embarrassment, and pain that has been brought by this one man, we hope by capturing the truth of Boris Johnson there is forever a permanent record of his shame so he cannot rewrite his legacy with more lies – for that would be a grave injustice.

NOTES

BORIS THE LYING JOURNALIST

JOHNSON'S FIRST LIE

[1] Anonymous, "Boris Johnson: I was wrong to make up a quote about King Edward II and his gay lover Piers Gaveston", *Pink News*, 26 March 2013, https://www.pinknews.co.uk/2013/03/26/boris-johnson-i-was-wrong-to-make-up-a-quote-about-king-edward-ii-and-his-gay-lover-piers-gaveston/

[2] Hogg, Clare Dwyer, "My greatest mistake: Boris Johnson, MP for Henley and editor of 'The Spectator'", *Independent*, 21 May 2002, https://www.independent.co.uk/news/media/my-greatest-mistake-boris-johnson-mp-for-henley-and-editor-of-the-spectator-189322.html

[3] Steerpike, "Revealed: Boris Johnson's Piers Gaveston porkies", *The Spectator*, 21 September 2015, https://www.spectator.co.uk/article/revealed-boris-johnson-s-piers-gaveston-porkies

[4] Bambridge, Steve, "The link between Boris Johnson and Scarborough's most famous ghost", *The Scarborough News*, 25 July 2019, https://www.thescarboroughnews.co.uk/news/people/link-between-boris-johnson-and-scarboroughs-most-famous-ghost-683638

[5] Hoggart, Simon, "Boris Johnson has been brought to his knees by a man who died in 1312", *The Guardian*, 25 March 2013, https://www.theguardian.com/politics/2013/mar/25/simon-hoggart-sketch-boris-johnson

LYING ABOUT EU COFFIN SIZES

[1] Johnson, Boris, *Lend Me Your Ears*, London: HarperCollins UK

[2] Barnes, Peter, "Reality Check: Does the EU limit coffin sizes?" BBC News, 23 March 2016, https://www.bbc.com/news/uk-politics-eu-referendum-35886338

[3] Council of Europe, "Agreement on the Transfer of Corpses", 26 October 1973, https://rm.coe.int/168007617d

[4] Ashton, Emily, "Boris Johnson Accused Of 'Exaggerating' EU Rules To Make Case For Brexit", BuzzFeed News, 23 March 2016, https://www.buzzfeed.com/emilyashton/balloons-teabags-coffins

[5] Anonymous, "Boris Ticked Off Over 'Exaggerated' EU Claims", Sky News, 23 March 2016, https://news.sky.com/story/boris-ticked-off-over-exaggerated-eu-claims-10215533

LYING ABOUT THE HILLSBOROUGH TRAGEDY

[1] Johnson, Boris, "Bigley's fate", *The Spectator*, 16 October 2004, https://www.spectator.co.uk/article/bigley-s-fate

[2] Pickard-Whitehead, Gabrielle, "Reasons why the people of Liverpool cannot forgive Boris Johnson", Left Foot Forward, 21 May 2022, https://leftfootforward. org/2022/05/reasons-why-the-people-of-liverpool-cannot-forgive-boris-johnson/

[3] Evans, Tony, "Opinion: This is why Liverpool fans boo the national anthem and this is what would stop it", *Independent*, 17 May 2022, https:// www.independent.co.uk/sport/football/liver-pool-fans-anthem-boris-johnson-b2080656. html?utm_content=Echobox&utm_medium=So-cial&utm_source=Facebook&fbclid=IwAR3X-Cx-R2zSIoUsmHZsfWAAcXm9NCUYkyL9RImm__2eD-vFz6pC7MHS8e0T0#Echobox=1652798846

[4] Turner, Richard, "Five Hillsborough myths dispelled by inquests jury", BBC News, 28 April 2016, https://www. bbc.com/news/uk-england-merseyside-35473732

[5] Mulholland, Hélène, "Boris Johnson apologises for Hillsborough article", *The Guardian*, 13 September 2012, https://www.theguardian.com/football/2012/sep/13/ boris-johnson-apologises-hillsborough-article

[6] Thorp, Liam, "Boris Johnson brazenly refuses to apologise for Liverpool and Hillsborough slurs", *Liverpool Echo*, 25 July 2019, https://www.liverpoolecho. co.uk/news/liverpool-news/boris-johnson-brazenly-refus-es-apologise-16645338

BORIS THE LYING POLITICIAN

SACKED FOR LYING (AGAIN)

[1] *The Week*, "Why Boris Johnson was sacked from the shadow cabinet", *The Week*, 26 June 2019, https://www.theweek.co.uk/101963/why-boris-johnson-was-sacked-from-the-shadow-cabinet

[2] McSmith, Andy, "On your bike, Boris: Howard sacks Johnson over private life", Independent, 14 November 2004, https://www.independent.co.uk/news/uk/politics/on-your-bike-boris-howard-sacks-johnson-over-private-life-8004350.html

[3] Hinsliff, Gaby, "Boris Johnson sacked by Tories over private life", *The Guardian*, 14 November 2004, https://www.theguardian.com/politics/2004/nov/14/uk.conservatives

LYING TO HIS BOSS (AGAIN)

[1] Sabbagh, Dan & Perraudin, Frances, "Laughter and lies: Johnson's journey from journalist to MP", *The Guardian*, 15 July 2019, https://www.theguardian.com/politics/2019/jul/15/laughter-lies-boris-johnson-journey-journalist-mp

[2] Purnell, Sofia, *Just Boris*, London: Aurum, 2011, p.226

[3] Purnell, Sofia, *Just Boris*, London: Aurum, 2011, p.230

[4] Chakelian, Anoosh, "Boris Johnson denied at least 17 times that he would return to parliament in 2015", *The New Statesman*, 6 August 2014, https://www.newstatesman.com/politics/uk-politics/2014/08/

boris-johnson-denied-least-17-times-he-would-return-parliament-2015

[5] Wintour, Patrick, "Boris Johnson dismisses talk of becoming prime minister", *The Guardian*, 8 August 2012, https://www.theguardian.com/politics/2012/aug/08/boris-johnson-prime-minister-prat

LYING ABOUT THE GARDEN BRIDGE

[1] Garden Bridge Trust, "About the project", 2016, https://web.archive.org/web/20161017222203/https://www.gardenbridge.london/about-the-project

[2] Neate, Rupert & Addley, Esther, "'You pay for it, chum': Johnson's struggle to save his garden bridge", *The Guardian*, 16 July 2019, https://www.theguardian.com/politics/2019/jul/16/you-pay-for-it-chum-boris-johnson-struggle-save-garden-bridge

[3] Moore, Rowan, "London's Garden bridge: barking up the wrong tree?", *The Guardian*, 14 September 2014, https://www.theguardian.com/artanddesign/2014/sep/14/london-garden-bridge-barking-up-wrong-tree

[4] Ibid.

[5] Hurst, Will, "Garden Bridge construction contract risks 'downplayed' for Boris Johnson", *Construction News*, 15 October 2019, https://www.constructionnews.co.uk/civils/garden-bridge-construction-contract-risks-downplayed-boris-johnson-15-10-2019/

[6] Hurst, Will, "Are Boris Johnson's Garden Bridge claims true or false?", *Architects Journal*, 7 March 2018, https://

www.architectsjournal.co.uk/news/are-boris-johnsons-garden-bridge-claims-true-or-false

[7] Mance, Henry, "Boris Johnson unable to answer questions on Garden Bridge", *Financial Times*, 1 March 2018, https://www.ft.com/content/60913776-1d72-11e8-956a-43db76e69936

[8] Anonymous, "Failed London Garden Bridge project cost £53m", BBC News, 13 February 2019, https://www.bbc.co.uk/news/uk-england-london-47228698

LYING ABOUT HIS CRONYISM

[1] Mulholland, Hélène, "Boris Johnson pressed for full details of the appointment of his alleged lover", *The Guardian*, 20 July 2010, https://www.theguardian.com/politics/2010/jul/20/boris-johnson-mayor-2012-macintyre

[2] Anonymous, "Boris Johnson faces probe over job for 'ex-lover'", *Evening Standard*, 12 April 2012, https://www.standard.co.uk/hp/front/boris-johnson-faces-probe-over-job-for-exlover-6541507.html

[3] Mulholland, Hélène, "No censure for Boris Johnson over relationship with unpaid City Hall adviser", *The Guardian*, 15 December 2010, https://www.theguardian.com/politics/2010/dec/15/no-censure-boris-johnson-city-hall-adviser

[4] Anonymous, "Boris Johnson challenged over Jennifer Arcuri relationship", BBC News, 20 April 2021, https://www.bbc.co.uk/news/uk-politics-56818748

[5] Townsend, Mark, "Fresh revelations about Jennifer Arcuri affair threaten to damage Boris Johnson", *The Guardian*, 29 January 2022, https://www.theguardian.com/politics/2022/jan/29/fresh-revelations-about-jennifer-arcuri-affair-threaten-to-damage-boris-johnson

[6] GLA Oversight Committee, "Governance of Trade Missions and the GLA Code of Conduct", London Assembly, September 2022, https://www.london.gov.uk/sites/default/files/governance_of_trade_missions_and_the_gla_code_of_conduct.pdf

LYING ABOUT LONDON'S CHALLENGES

[1] Johnson, Boris, "Safer roads for cycling across London", London Assembly, 14 March 2012, https://www.london.gov.uk/questions/2012/1030

[2] Anonymous, "Has cycling got safer under Boris Johnson?", Full Fact, 13 April 2012, https://fullfact.org/news/has-cycling-got-safer-under-boris-johnson/

[3] Jones, Sam, Weaver, Matthew, Walker, Peter & Wintour, Patrick, "Boris Johnson says cyclists must obey law after fifth death in nine days", *The Guardian*, 14 November 2013, https://www.theguardian.com/uk-news/2013/nov/14/fifth-london-bike-death-bus-superhighway

[4] Walker, Peter, "Boris Johnson blames cycling victims and ignores the bull in the china shop", *The Guardian*, 14 November 2013, https://www.theguardian.com/commentisfree/2013/nov/14/boris-johnson-blames-victims-cycling

[5] Mulholland, Hélène, "Boris Johnson sets out plans for green London", *The Guardian*, 25 November 2012, https://www.theguardian.com/politics/2008/nov/25/boris-green-politics

[6] Nicholson, Kate, "6 Times Boris Johnson Revealed His Climate Change Scepticism", The Huffington Post, 20 September 2021, https://www.huffingtonpost.co.uk/entry/boris-johnson-climate-change-sceptic_uk_61486d12e4b0e5dd4b294549

[7] Johnson, Boris, "The man who repeatedly beats the Met Office at its own game", *The Telegraph*, 19 December 2010, https://www.telegraph.co.uk/politics/0/man-repeatedly-beats-met-office-game/

[8] Ward, Bob, "Boris Johnson's climate change 'scepticism' is an embarrassment to London's scientists", *The New Statesman*, https://www.newstatesman.com/politics/2013/01/boris-johnsons-climate-change-scepticism-embarrassment-londons-scientists

[9] Anonymous, "Has Boris Johnson saved every Londoner £445?", Full Fact, 7 March 2012, https://fullfact.org/news/has-boris-johnson-saved-every-londoner-445/

LYING ABOUT TUBE STATION TICKET OFFICES

[1] Anonymous, "Boris's Broken Commitment To Keep All Ticket Offices Open", RMT London Calling, 1 May 2014, https://www.rmtlondoncalling.org.uk/content/boriss-broken-commitment-keep-all-ticket-offices-open

[2] Ackermann, Will, "Boris Johnson defends plans to axe rail ticket offices despite pledge not to", My London,

5 December 2014, https://www.mylondon.news/news/local-news/boris-johnson-defends-plans-axe-8234055

[3] Anonymous, "London's Tube and bus fares to rise by 4.2%", BBC News, 8 November 2012, https://www.bbc.co.uk/news/av/uk-england-london-20249561

[4] Major, Kirsty, "Why are we so surprised that Boris Johnson lied when he's been sacked for lying twice before?", Independent, 27 June 2016, https://www.independent.co.uk/voices/why-are-we-so-surprised-that-boris-johnson-lied-when-he-s-been-sacked-for-lying-twice-before-a7105976.html

LYING ABOUT SUPPORT FOR THE UNHOUSED

[1] Hill, Dave, "Rough sleeping in London is soaring – what was that pledge, Boris Johnson?", *The Guardian*, 14 December 2012, https://www.theguardian.com/commentisfree/2012/dec/14/rough-sleeping-london-soaring-boris-johnson

[2] Barrell, Ryan, "Boris Johnson's Promise To End London Homelessness By 2012 Mocked As Rough Sleeper Numbers Double", The Huffington Post UK, 1 January 2016, https://www.huffingtonpost.co.uk/2016/01/01/boris-johnson-homelessness-in-london-by-2012-numbers_n_8902358.html

LYING ABOUT SUPPORT FOR VICTIMS OF SEXUAL VIOLENCE

[1] Anonymous, "Boris backtracks on rape manifesto commitment", Politics.co.uk, 19 December 2008, https://www.politics.co.uk/news/2008/12/19/boris-back-tracks-on-rape-manifesto-commitment/

[2] Mullholland, Hélène, "Boris Johnson urged to honour rape crisis centres pledge", *The Guardian*, 21 October 2009, https://www.theguardian.com/politics/2009/oct/21/boris-johnson-rape-crisis-centres

LYING ABOUT HIS OWN RECORD AS MAYOR

[1] Johnson, Boris, "Question Time Leaders Special Live From Sheffield 22/11/2019", BBC News, 22 November 2019 https://www.youtube.com/watch?v=8cQMzVjHBeI

[2] Apps, Peter, "Fact check: did Boris Johnson 'massively outbuild Labour' as London mayor?" *Inside Housing*, 26 November 2019, https://www.insidehousing.co.uk/insight/insight/fact-check-did-boris-johnson-massively-outbuild-labour-as-london-mayor-64282

[3] Courea, Eleni, "Boris Johnson fact check: a record that is not quite as bright as claimed", *The Times*, 12 June 2019, https://www.thetimes.co.uk/article/boris-johnson-a-record-that-is-not-quite-as-bright-as-claimed-dgjlqdzv2

LYING ABOUT STOP AND SEARCH

[1] Yesufu, Shaka, "Discriminatory Use of Stop-and-Search Powers in London, UK", *International Journal of Police Science and Management*, 1 December 2013, 15(4), 281–293, https://doi.org/10.1350/ijps.2013.15.4.318

[2] Lee, Georgina, "Boris Johnson's stop and search knife claim", Channel 4 FactCheck, 20 August 2019, https://www.channel4.com/news/factcheck/factcheck-boris-johnsons-stop-and-search-knife-claim

[3] Johnson, Boris, "Boris Johnson makes first Commons statement as PM", BBC News, 25 July 2019, https://www.youtube.com/watch?v=aTQYvbZUGS8

[4] McCandless, Rhydian et al., "Do initiatives involving substantial increases in stop and search reduce crime?", Home Office, March 2016, https://assets.publishing.service.gov.uk/government/uploads/system/uploads/attachment_data/file/508661/stop-search-operation-blunt-2.pdf

[5] Buchan, Lizzy, "Boris Johnson under fire over incorrect claims about London murder rates during first Commons speech", *Independent*, 26 July 2019, https://www.independent.co.uk/news/uk/politics/boris-johnson-london-murder-crime-rate-incorrect-commons-speech-a9020826.html

[6] Walker, Peter, "Was Boris Johnson as successful as London mayor as he claims?", *The Guardian*, 12 June 2019, https://www.theguardian.com/politics/2019/jun/12/was-boris-johnson-as-successful-as-london-mayor-as-he-claims

[7] Milne, Oliver, "Boris Johnson's story about crying when his bike was nicked doesn't add up", *The Mirror*, 17 July 2019, https://www.mirror.co.uk/news/politics/boris-johnsons-story-crying-bike-18330557

[8] Johnson, Boris, "Riding my broken bike is like working with the Lib Dems", *The Telegraph*, 16 February 2014, https://www.telegraph.co.uk/news/politics/10642745/Riding-my-broken-bike-is-like-working-with-the-Lib-Dems.html

BORIS THE LYING BREXITEER

LYING ABOUT "BENDY BANANAS"

[1] Sparrow, Andrew, "Chaos in Cardiff as Labour fails to win first minister vote – Politics live", *The Guardian*, 11 May 2016 https://www.theguardian.com/politics/blog/live/2016/may/11/pmqs-corbyn-cameron-osborne-boris-johnson-interview-politics-live?page=with:block-5732f7aee-4b0a3721d605505#block-5732f7aee4b0a3721d605505

[2] Fanta, Alexander, "The real story why 'bonkers Brussels' went bananas", EU Observer, 5 October 2020, https://euobserver.com/news/149607

[3] Anonymous, "Bendy Bananas – the Myth to end all Myths", European Parliament Liaison Office in the United Kingdom, 26 May 2016, https://www.europarl.europa.eu/unitedkingdom/en/news-and-press-releases/euromyths/bendybananas.html

[4] European Commission, "Commission Regulation (EC) No. 2257/94 of 16 September 1994 laying down quality standards for bananas", 20 September 1994, https://eur-lex.europa.eu/LexUriServ/LexUriServ.do?uri=CON-SLEG:1994R2257:20060217:EN:PDF

[5] Steichen, Rene, "Answer given by Mr Steichen on behalf of the Commission", European Commission, 16 December 1994, https://www.europarl.europa.eu/doceo/document/E-4-1994-2418-ASW_EN.html?redirect

LYING ABOUT LORRY SAFETY

[1] Shone, Emma, "Boris: EU membership stopped safer cabs", *Commercial Motor*, 6 June 2016, https://www.commercialmotor.com/news/boris-eu-membership-stopped-safer-cabs

[2] Anonymous, "Do EU rules prevent safer lorries?", Full Fact, 10 July 2018, https://fullfact.org/europe/eu-rules-safer-lorries/

LYING ABOUT CHILDREN BLOWING UP BALLOONS

[1] Harris, Simon, "EU bans children blowing up balloons, claims Boris", ITV News, 16 March 2016, https://www.itv.com/news/london/2016-03-16/eu-bans-children-blowing-up-balloons-claims-boris

LYING ABOUT THE EURO

[1] Anonymous, "Will the UK pay for future Eurozone bailouts?", Full Fact, 22 June 2016, https://fullfact.org/europe/will-uk-pay-future-eurozone-bailouts/

LYING ABOUT TRAINS

[1] Anonymous, "Reality Check: Boris Johnson's claims about the EU", BBC News, 9 May 2016, https://www.bbc.co.uk/news/uk-politics-eu-referendum-35959948

LYING ABOUT THE NHS ON THE SIDE OF A BUS

[1] Full Fact Team, "£350 million EU claim 'a clear misuse of official statistics'", Full Fact, 19 September 2017, https://fullfact.org/europe/350-million-week-boris-johnson-statistics-authority-misuse/

[2] Lichfield, John, "Boris Johnson's £350m claim is devious and bogus. Here's why", *The Guardian*, 18 September 2017, https://www.theguardian.com/commentisfree/2017/sep/18/boris-johnson-350-million-claim-bogus-foreign-secretary

[3] Stone, Jon, "British public still believe Vote Leave '£350million a week to EU' myth from Brexit referendum", *Independent*, 28 October 2018, https://www.independent.co.uk/news/uk/politics/vote-leave-brexit-lies-eu-pay-money-remain-poll-boris-johnson-a8603646.html

[4] Cummings, Dominic, "Dominic Cummings: how the Brexit referendum was won", *The Spectator*, 9 January 2017, https://www.spectator.co.uk/article/dominic-cummings-how-the-brexit-referendum-was-won

LYING ABOUT TURKEY'S FUTURE MEMBERSHIP OF THE EU

[1] Carl, Dr Noah, "People's stated reasons for voting leave or remain", UK in a Changing Europe, 31 July 2018, https://ukandeu.ac.uk/partner-reports/peoples-stated-reasons-for-voting-leave-or-remain/

[2] Smith, Matthew, "Turkey less popular choice to join the EU than even Russia", YouGov, 3 August 2016, https://yougov.co.uk/topics/politics/articles-reports/2016/08/03/turkey-less-popular-choice-join-eu-even-russia

[3] Johnson, Boris, "Boris: UK population will rise 'inexorably' if we stay in EU", BBC *Andrew Marr Show*, 5 June 2016, https://www.bbc.co.uk/programmes/p03xbz9g

[4] Stubley, Peter, "Boris Johnson: The most infamous lies and untruths by the Conservative leadership candidate", *Independent*, 25 May 2019, https://www.independent.co.uk/news/uk/politics/boris-johnson-lies-conservative-leader-candidate-list-times-banana-brexit-bus-a8929076.html

[5] Full Fact Team, "Is Turkey likely to join the EU?", Full Fact, 26 May 2016, https://fullfact.org/europe/turkey-likely-join-eu/

[6] Stewart, Heather, & Mason, Rowena, "Nigel Farage's anti-migrant poster reported to police", *The Guardian*, 16 June 2016, https://www.theguardian.com/politics/2016/jun/16/nigel-farage-defends-ukip-breaking-point-poster-queue-of-migrants

[7] Sabbagh, Dan & Rankin, Jennifer, "Boris Johnson wrongly denies stirring Turkey fears in Brexit campaign", *The Guardian*, 18 January 2019

[8] Johnson, Boris, "Boris: UK population will rise 'inexorably' if we stay in EU", BBC *Andrew Marr Show*, 5 June 2016, https://www.bbc.co.uk/programmes/p03xbz9g

[9] Warrall, Patrick, "Boris Johnson falsely claims he 'didn't say anything about Turkey' in the referendum campaign", Channel 4 FactCheck, 18 January 2019, https://www.channel4.com/news/factcheck/factcheck-boris-johnson-falsely-claims-he-didnt-say-anything-about-turkey-in-the-referendum-campaign

ELECTION LIES, IMAGINARY ACCOMPLISHMENTS, AND COVID-19

LYING ABOUT HIS REASONS FOR SEEKING OFFICE

[1] *The Week*, "The six times Boris Johnson has denied that he wants to be Prime Minister", *The Week*, 12 June 2017, https://www.theweek.co.uk/85515/the-six-times-boris-johnson-has-denied-he-wants-to-be-prime-minister

[2] Bienkov, Alex, Colson, Thomas, & Payne, Adam, "Boris Johnson calls for a snap general election on December 12 to 'get Brexit done'", Business Insider, 24 October 2019, https://www.businessinsider.com/boris-johnson-calls-for-a-snap-general-election-on-december-12-2019-10?r=US&IR=T

[3] Peck, Tom, "Boris Johnson launched the Conservative election campaign today with a sewer of lies",

Independent, 6 November 2019, https://www.independent.co.uk/voices/boris-johnson-election-tory-party-conservative-brexit-nhs-hospitals-a9188531.html

[4] Walters, Simon, "Wallpapergate: Leaked £200,000 list reveals Boris Johnson's flat renovation plans included £7,000 rug and £3,675 trolley", *Independent*, 7 July 2022, https://www.independent.co.uk/news/uk/politics/boris-johnson-wallpaper-gold-flat-carrie-invoice-b2118185.html

[5] Fletcher, Martin, "Boris Johnson's resignation honours list will be the final insult", *The New Statesman*, n.d., https://www.newstatesman.com/comment/2022/09/boris-johnson-resignation-honours-list-last-insult

[6] Elgot, Jessica, "Secret Boris Johnson column favoured UK remaining in EU", *The Guardian*, 16 October 2016, https://www.theguardian.com/politics/2016/oct/16/secret-boris-johnson-column-favoured-uk-remaining-in-eu

[7] Settle, Michael, "David Cameron: Boris Johnson 'didn't believe' in Brexit and only backed Leave campaign to further his career", *The Herald*, 15 September 2019, https://www.heraldscotland.com/news/17903645.david-cameron-boris-johnson-didnt-believe-brexit-backed-leave-campaign-career/

LYING ABOUT THE ECONOMY

[1] Panjwani, Abbas, "UK is fastest growing G7 economy by one measure, and fifth by another", Full Fact, 13 January 2022, https://fullfact.org/economy/january-2022-gdp-growth-g7/

[2] Goodman, David, "UK Economy Shrank Most Since 1709 in Pandemic as Numbers Revised Again", Bloomberg UK, 22 August 2022, https://www.bloomberg.com/news/articles/2022-08-22/uk-shrank-most-since-1709-in-pandemic-as-numbers-revised-again#xj4y7vzkg

[3] Full Fact Team, "The ITV Boris Johnson vs Jeremy Corbyn debate, fact checked", Full Fact, 19 November 2019, https://fullfact.org/election-2019/itv-boris-johnson-jeremy-corbyn-debate-fact-checked/

[4] Benedictus, Leo, "Was Dawn Butler right about Boris Johnson 'lying' to Parliament?", Full Fact, 23 July 2021, https://fullfact.org/news/dawn-butler-boris-johnson-lying/

LYING ABOUT POVERTY

[1] Butcher, Ben, 'Child Poverty: Boris Johnson's claims fact-checked', BBC News, 29 June 2020, https://www.bbc.co.uk/news/53181798

LYING ABOUT CRIME

[1] Carmichael, Alistair, 'Letter to Sir David Norgrove – Use of official crime statistics by Prime Minister, Home Secretary, and Home Office', Parliamentary Correspondence, 3 February 2022, https://uksa.statisticsauthority.gov.uk/correspondence/alistair-carmichael-mp-to-sir-david-norgrove-use-of-official-crime-statistics-by-prime-minister-home-secretary-and-home-office/

LYING ABOUT COVID-19 TEST AND TRACE

[1] Cowburn, Ashley, ''Rubbish': Boris Johnson accused of misleading claim that no other country has 'functioning test and trace app'', Independent, 23 June 2020, https://www.independent.co.uk/news/uk/politics/boris-johnson-test-and-trace-app-coronavirus-uk-germany-a9581146.html

LYING ABOUT CLIMATE VICTORIES

[1] Rigby, Beth, "COP26: Boris Johnson admits it's 'going to be a stretch' to secure climate promises", Sky News, 20 September 2021, https://news.sky.com/story/cop26-boris-johnson-admits-its-going-to-be-a-stretch-to-secure-100bn-in-climate-pledges-12412636

[2] Snaith, Emma, "Boris Johnson refuses to take part in climate debate, despite UN's dire environmental warning", *Independent*, 26 November 2019, https://www.independent.co.uk/climate-change/news/boris-johnson-climate-change-debate-channel-4-general-election-un-a9218441.html

[3] Weston, Phoebe, "Scientists deride Johnson's claim UK on 'verge' of creating commercial nuclear fusion reactors", *Independent*, 2 October 2019, https://www.independent.co.uk/climate-change/news/boris-johnson-conservative-party-conference-commercial-fusion-reactors-a9130821.html

LYING ABOUT GETTING "THE BIG CALLS RIGHT"

[1] Dunt, Ian, "Apparently Boris Johnson 'got the big calls right'. Nothing could be further from the truth", iNews, 7 July 2022, https://inews.co.uk/opinion/apparently-boris-johnson-got-the-big-calls-right-nothing-could-be-further-from-the-truth-1729658

[2] Helm, Toby, Inman, Phillip, & Tapper, James, "'We got all the big calls right' said Boris Johnson. But did he really?", *The Guardian*, 30 January 2022, https://www.theguardian.com/politics/2022/jan/30/we-got-the-big-calls-right-said-boris-johnson-but-did-he-really

LYING ABOUT "GETTING BREXIT DONE"

[1] Jenkins, Simon, "'Get Brexit Done' is this election's biggest lie", *The Guardian*, 9 December 2019, https://www.theguardian.com/commentisfree/2019/dec/09/get-brexit-done-lie-leave-eu-johnson

[2] O'Toole, Fintan, "Britain's attack on its own protocol is one more exercise in Brexit gaslighting", *The Guardian*, 15 June 2022, https://www.theguardian.com/commentisfree/2022/jun/15/britain-ni-protocol-brexit-ministers-deal

LYING TO THE QUEEN ABOUT PROROGATION

[1] Crerar, Pippa, "Queen 'will not be amused' after Boris Johnson 'lied' about prorogation motive", *The Mirror*, 11 September 2019, https://www.mirror.co.uk/news/politics/queen-will-not-amused-after-20044814

[2] Allen Green, David, "Scottish judges decide Boris Johnson misled the Queen", *Financial Times*, 11 September 2019, https://www.ft.com/content/12097e7c-d47f-11e9-8367-807ebd53ab77

[3] Davis, Fergal, "Decision of the Supreme Court on the Prorogation of Parliament", House of Commons Library, 24 September 2019, https://commonslibrary.parliament.uk/decision-of-the-supreme-court-on-the-prorogation-of-parliament/

[4] MacAskill, Andrew, & Faulconbridge, Guy, "'Absolutely Not': PM Johnson denies lying to Queen Elizabeth in Brexit Crisis", Reuters, 12 September, 2019, https://www.reuters.com/article/us-britain-eu-idUSKCN-1VX0W3

[5] Merrick, Rob, & Rahim, Zamira, "Boris Johnson forced to cut short US trip and fly back to parliament after humiliating Supreme Court ruling", *Independent*, 24 September 2019, https://www.independent.co.uk/news/uk/politics/boris-johnson-news-latest-un-speech-parliament-return-brexit-supreme-court-ruling-a9118271.html

[6] David, David, "Be warned: this government is robbing you of your right to challenge the state", *The Guardian*, 25 October 2021, https://www.theguardian.com/commentisfree/2021/oct/25/judicial-review-peoples-right-fight-government-destroy-courts-undemocratic

LYING ABOUT HIS COVID-19 RESPONSE

[1] Rogers, Paul, "The flailing PM is rewriting history to claim 'COVID success'. Don't let him", openDemocracy, 11 June 2022, https://www.opendemocracy.net/en/boris-johnson-covid-success-uk-2020-failures/

[2] Cusick, James, & Geoghegan, Peter, "Tory billionaire bankrolled 'herd immunity' scientist who advised PM against lockdown", openDemocracy, 9 April 2021, https://www.opendemocracy.net/en/dark-money-investigations/tory-billionaire-bankrolled-herd-immunity-scientist-who-advised-pm-against-lockdown/

[3] Aschwanden, Christie, "The false promise of herd immunity for COVID-19", *Nature*, 21 October 2020, https://www.nature.com/articles/d41586-020-02948-4

[3] Yong, Ed, "The U.K.'s Coronavirus 'Herd Immunity' debacle", *The Atlantic*, 16 March 2020, https://www.theatlantic.com/health/archive/2020/03/coronavirus-pandemic-herd-immunity-uk-boris-johnson/608065/

[4] Freedland, Jonathan, "Don't call it sleaze, call it corruption – why scandal haunts Boris Johnson's government", *The Guardian*, 16 December 2021, https://www.theguardian.com/politics/2021/dec/16/dont-call-it-sleaze-call-it-corruption-why-scandal-haunts-boris-johnsons-government

[5] Our World In Data, "United Kingdom: Coronavirus Pandemic Country Profile", Our World In Data, 29 September 2022, https://ourworldindata.org/coronavirus/country/united-kingdom

[6] Sridhar, Devi, "As Covid deaths in the UK pass the grim milestone of 200,000, what have we learned?", *The Guardian*, 13 July 2022, https://www.theguardian.com/commentisfree/2022/jul/13/as-covid-deaths-in-the-uk-surpass-the-grim-milestone-of-200000-what-have-we-learned

[7] Reuters, "UK PM's former advisor confirms Johnson said 'let the bodies pile high'", Reuters, 26 May 2021, https://www.reuters.com/world/uk/uk-pms-former-adviser-confirms-johnson-said-let-bodies-pile-high-2021-05-26/

LYING ABOUT THE VACCINE ROLLOUT

[1] Reality Check Team, "PMQs: Fact-checking claims on fraud, Brexit, and the economy", BBC News, 9 February 2022, https://www.bbc.co.uk/news/60305472

[2] BBC, "Covid vaccines: how fast is progress around the world?", BBC News, 1 June 2022, https://www.bbc.co.uk/news/world-56237778

[3] Morris, Chris, "UK vaccine approval: did Brexit speed up the process?", BBC News, 2 December 2020, https://www.bbc.co.uk/news/55163730

"GLOBAL BRITAIN": FOREIGN POLICY AND MORE BREXIT

LYING ABOUT REFUGEES AND ASYLUM SEEKERS

[1] Asthana, Anushka, "Is the UK as 'generous' as Boris Johnson claims it is with regards to refugees?", ITV News, 1 March 2022, https://www.itv.com/news/2022-03-01/is-the-uk-really-very-generous-when-it-comes-to-refugees

[2] Reality Check Team, "Fact-Checking Boris Johnson's claim about refugees", BBC News, 9 March 2022, https://www.bbc.co.uk/news/60679290

[3] Bryant, Miranda, & Townsend, Mark, "50,000 Ukrainian Refugees in UK facing homelessness 'disaster' next year", *The Guardian*, 28 August 2022, https://www.theguardian.com/world/2022/aug/28/50000-ukrainian-refugees-in-uk-facing-homeless-ness-disaster-next-year-homes-for-ukraine

[4] Balch, Alex, "Nationality and Borders Act becomes law: five key changes explained", The Conversation, 29 April 2022, https://theconversation.com/nationality-and-borders-act-becomes-law-five-key-chang-es-explained-182099

[5] Peat, Jack, "'Lefty-lawyers are spoiling our Rwanda plan', PM says", The London Economic, 5 May 2022, https://www.thelondoneconomic.com/politics/lefty-law-yers-are-spoiling-our-rwanda-plan-pm-says-321623/

LYING ABOUT FOREIGN INTERFERENCE IN ELECTIONS

[1] Woodcock, Andrew, "Boris Johnson falsely claims there is 'no evidence' of Russian interference in UK politics", *Independent*, 15 November 2019, https://www.independent.co.uk/news/uk/politics/boris-johnson-russia-report-interference-brexit-general-election-a9204051.html

[2] Bienkov, Adam, "Boris Johnson's Lies are Turning the UK into a Global Embarrassment", Byline Times, 1 February 2022, https://bylinetimes.com/2022/02/01/boris-johnsons-party-lies-are-turning-the-uk-into-a-global-embarrassment/

[3] Cusick, James, "Number 10 abused its power by demanding cover-up of donors and friends of Boris in report on Russian influence", openDemocracy, 11 November 2019, https://www.opendemocracy.net/en/dark-money-investigations/number-10-abused-its-power-demanding-cover-donors-and-friends-boris-report-russian-influence/

[4] Sabbagh, Dan, "MPs to question chair of appointments panel over Evgeny Lebedev peerage", *The Guardian*, 13 April 2022, https://www.theguardian.com/politics/2022/apr/13/mps-to-question-chair-of-appointments-panel-over-evgeny-lebedev-peerage

LYING ABOUT NORTHERN IRELAND AND BREXIT

[1] *The Irish News*, "The Story of the Irish Sea Border in Six Quotes", *The Irish News*, 10 December 2020, https://www.irishnews.com/news/

northernirelandnews/2020/12/10/news/the-story-of-the-irish-sea-border-in-six-quotes-2155761/

[2] BBC News, "Brexit: What is the Northern Ireland Protocol?", BBC News, 27 June 2022, https://www.bbc.co.uk/news/explainers-53724381

[3] Reality Check Team, "Northern Ireland Protocol: What did Boris Johnson say?", BBC News, 14 June 2022, https://www.bbc.co.uk/news/58001530

[4] Mason, Rowena, & Boffey, Daniel, "EU poised to take legal action against UK over Northern Ireland Protocol Bill", 13 June 2022, https://www.theguardian.com/uk-news/2022/jun/13/uk-risks-brexit-eu-trade-war-as-northern-ireland-protocol-bill-is-published

[5] McAllister, David, Lange, Bernd, & Loiseau, Nathalie, "Serious breach of international law: MEPs call on UK not to adopt new bill", EU Parliament Press Room, 14 June 2022, https://www.europarl.europa.eu/news/en/press-room/20220614IPR32901/serious-breach-of-international-law-meps-call-on-uk-not-to-adopt-new-bill

[6] O'Toole, Fintan, "Britain's attack on its own protocol is one more exercise in Brexit gaslighting", *The Guardian*, 15 June 2022, https://www.theguardian.com/commentisfree/2022/jun/15/britain-ni-protocol-brexit-ministers-deal

LYING ABOUT THE IMPACT OF BREXIT

[1] Worrall, Patrick, "Footage appears to contradict Boris Johnson's claim of only 170 lorries near Dover", Channel 4, 22 December 2020, https://www.channel4.com/news/

factcheck/factcheck-footage-appears-to-contradict-boris-johnsons-claim-of-only-170-lorries-near-dover

[2] Parker, George, & Giles, Chris, "The deafening silence over Brexit's economic fallout", *Financial Times*, 20 June 2022,

https://www.ft.com/content/7a209a34-7d95-47aa-91b0-bf02d4214764

[3] Jenkins, Simon, "There is one man to blame for the lorries backed up in Dover: Boris Johnson", *The Guardian*, 25 July 2022, https://www.theguardian.com/commentisfree/2022/jul/25/lorries-dover-boris-johnson-tory-leadership-brexit

[4] Statista, "In hindsight, do you think Britain was right or wrong to leave the European Union?", Statista Politics & Government, 5 August 2022, https://www.statista.com/statistics/987347/brexit-opinion-poll/

[5] Mason, Paul, "There will be no UK-US trade deal – and the Brexit fantasy has been punctured", *The New Statesman*, 21 September 2022, https://www.newstatesman.com/comment/2022/09/no-uk-us-trade-deal-brexit-fantasy

[6] Russell-Jones, Lily, "Boris Johnson plans to cut EU red tape in boost to post-Brexit economy", City AM, 9 May 2022, https://www.cityam.com/boris-johnson-plans-to-cut-eu-red-tape-in-boost-to-post-brexit-economy/

LYING ABOUT THE EUROPEAN CONVENTION ON HUMAN RIGHTS

[1] Webber, Esther, "Boris Johnson rages at European Court of Human Rights. But will he act?", Politico, 16 June 2022, https://www.politico.eu/article/uk-boris-johnson-slams-the-european-court-of-human-rights-but-will-he-act/

[2] Equality and Human Rights Commission, "What is the European Convention on Human Rights?", Equality and Human Rights Commission, 19 April 2017, https://www.equalityhumanrights.com/en/what-european-convention-human-rights

[3] Liberty, "The Human Rights Act", Liberty Human Rights, 30 September 2022, https://www.libertyhumanrights.org.uk/your-rights/the-human-rights-act/#:~:text=are%20under%20threat-,What%20is%20the%20Human%20Rights%20Act%3F,with%20fairness%2C%20dignity%20and%20respect.

[4] The Law Society, "Human Rights Act reforms and the Bill of Rights Bill", Law Society Human Rights, 28 September 2022, https://www.lawsociety.org.uk/topics/human-rights/human-rights-act-reforms

PERSONAL CONDUCT, POLITICAL SMEARS, AND SCANDALS

LYING ABOUT HIS OWN CONDUCT

[1] ITV News, "Boris Johnson tells ITV News he would 'walk away' from US trade deal talks if NHS put on the table", ITV News, 28 November 2019, https://www.itv.com/news/2019-11-28/boris-johnson-tells-itv-news-he-would-walk-away-from-us-trade-talks-if-nhs-put-on-table

[2] Stewart, Heather, "Boris Johnson: MPs should be punished for breaking the rules", *The Guardian*, 10 November 2021, https://www.theguardian.com/politics/2021/nov/10/boris-johnson-mps-should-be-punished-for-breaking-the-rules

[3] Mason, Rowena, & Allegretti, Aubrey, "Boris Johnson accused of changing ministerial code to 'save his skin'", *The Guardian*, 27 May 2022, https://www.theguardian.com/politics/2022/may/27/boris-johnson-changes-ministerial-code-to-remove-need-to-resign-over-breaches

[4] Heffer, Greg, "Boris vows to take 'full responsibility' if Tories suffer a local elections hammering after Partygate as PM promises to show 'compassion' during cost-of-living crisis and telling Britons it 'will get better'", *The Daily Mail*, 3 May 2022, https://www.dailymail.co.uk/news/article-10779527/Boris-Johnson-responsibility-Tory-local-elections-hammering-Partygate.html

LYING ABOUT POLITICAL SMEARS

[1] Partington, Richard, "How accurate were Johnson's Andrew Marr interview claims?", *The Guardian*, 1 December 2019, https://www.theguardian.com/politics/2019/dec/01/how-accurate-were-boris-johnsons-assertions-on-andrew-marr

[2] Abraham, Ellie, "Who won today's PMQs? Johnson uses 'Vladimir Corbyn' jibe as Starmer points to government U-turn", *The Guardian*, 25 May 2022, https://www.indy100.com/politics/pmqs-johnson-starmer-sue-gray

[3] Bienkov, Adam, "Boris Johnson's Lies are Turning the UK into a Global Embarrassment", Byline Times, 1 February 2022, https://bylinetimes.com/2022/02/01/boris-johnsons-party-lies-are-turning-the-uk-into-a-global-embarrassment/

[4] Turnnidge, Sarah, "Keir Starmer hasn't voted 48 times to take the UK back into the EU", Full Fact, 23 February 2022, https://fullfact.org/europe/keir-starmer-48-votes-brexit/

[5] Plummer, Kate, "Even Dominic Raab appeared unimpressed with Johnson's 'Beer Korma' joke", indy100, 26 May 2022, https://www.indy100.com/politics/dominic-raab-beer-korma-johnson

[6] Payne, Sebastian, "Keir Starmer cleared after UK police complete 'beergate' probe", *Financial Times*, 8 July 2022, https://www.ft.com/content/3e1f2773-8503-4710-83b7-95a41530c00a

LYING ABOUT ALMOST EVERYTHING

[1] Clifton, Katy, "Boris Johnson defends Dominic Cummings after 'lockdown breach' as he claims top aid acted with 'integrity'", *Evening Standard*, 24 May 2020, https://www.standard.co.uk/news/uk/boris-johnson-defend-dominic-cummings-lockdown-a4449701.html

[2] Weaver, Matthew, "Dominic Cummings: Durham police reject dossier of evidence on lockdown journeys", *The Guardian*, 5 February 2021, https://www.standard.co.uk/news/uk/boris-johnson-defend-dominic-cummings-lockdown-a4449701.html

[3] BBC, "Cummings drove to Barnard Castle 'to 'test vision'", BBC News, 25 May 2020, https://www.bbc.co.uk/news/av/uk-52801667

[4] Webber, Esther, "Boris Johnson defends handling of disgraced health secretary's exit", Politico, 28 June 2021, https://www.politico.eu/article/boris-johnson-defends-handling-of-disgraced-health-secretarys-exit/

[5] Walker, Peter, "Boris Johnson wrongly cleared over Covid contracts, say MPs", *The Guardian*, 4 May 2021, https://www.theguardian.com/politics/2021/may/04/boris-johnson-wrongly-cleared-over-covid-contracts-say-mps

[6] Siddique, Haroon, "Use of 'VIP lane' to award Covid PPE contracts unlawful, high court rules", *The Guardian*, 12 January 2022, https://www.theguardian.com/politics/2022/jan/12/use-of-vip-lane-to-award-covid-ppe-contracts-unlawful-high-court-rules

[7] Sky News, "Boris Johnson tried to water down Priti Patel bullying report, say Whitehall sources", Sky

News, 21 November 2020, https://news.sky.com/story/boris-johnson-tried-to-water-down-priti-patel-bullying-report-say-whitehall-sources-12137960

[8] Walker, Peter, "Boris Johnson admits defending Owen Paterson was a 'total mistake'", *The Guardian*, 17 November 2021, https://www.theguardian.com/politics/2021/nov/17/boris-johnson-admits-defending-owen-paterson-was-total-mistake

LYING ABOUT PARTYING, THEN LYING ABOUT PARTYGATE

[1] Buchan, Lizzy, & Bloom, Dan, "All Boris Johnson's Partygate denials in his own words – how the PM 'repeatedly lied'", *The Mirror*, 25 May 2022, https://www.mirror.co.uk/news/politics/boris-johnsons-partygate-denials-words-26696780

[2] Walker, Peter, Allegretti, Aubrey, & Grierson, Jamie, "PM accused of lying after No 10 officials caught joking about Christmas party", *The Guardian*, 7 December 2021, https://www.theguardian.com/politics/2021/dec/07/leaked-video-shows-no-10-officials-joking-about-holding-christmas-party

[3] Badshah, Nadeem, "Downing Street accused of trying to 'dilute' Sue Gray's Partygate report", *The Guardian*, 29 May 2022, https://www.theguardian.com/politics/2022/may/29/downing-street-reportedly-tried-to-get-partygate-report-diluted

[4] Walker, Peter, "Sue Gray report: full breakdown of findings about No 10 parties", *The Guardian*, 25 May 2022, https://www.theguardian.com/politics/2022/

may/25/sue-gray-report-full-breakdown-findings-no-10-parties

[5] Wearmouth, Rachel, "BBC confronts Tory over government cleaner who died after Partygate 'disrespect'", *The Mirror*, 26 May 2022, https://www.mirror.co.uk/news/politics/bbc-confronts-tory-over-government-27070516

LYING ABOUT PROMOTING A SEX PEST — THE ONE THAT GOT HIM IN THE END

[1] Sky News, "What did Boris Johnson know about Chris Pincher groping claims and when? Here's what Downing Street has said", Sky News, 5 July 2022, https://news.sky.com/story/what-did-boris-johnson-know-about-chris-pincher-groping-claims-and-when-heres-what-downing-street-has-said-12646152

[2] Merrick, Rob, "PMQs: Boris Johnson fails to deny saying 'Pincher by name, pincher by nature' about ex-minister", *Independent*, 6 July 2022, https://www.independent.co.uk/news/uk/politics/boris-johnson-pmqs-pincher-starmer-b2116966.html

[3] Morris, Sophie, "Chris Pincher refuses to answer questions following Boris Johnson's downfall", Sky News, 29 July 2022, https://news.sky.com/story/chris-pincher-refuses-to-answer-questions-in-awkward-exchange-following-boris-johnsons-downfall-12661281

ABOUT THE AUTHOR

Kyle Taylor is also the author of *The Little Black Book of Data and Democracy*, an easy-to-read, accessibly guide to how big tech is undermining democracy that became an instant hit with readers around the world. He is the Founder of Fair Vote UK, which has spent the last half-decade working to hold lying politicians like Boris Johnson to account. He is an expert on elections, digital democracy and disinformation. Kyle has worked on half-a dozen election campaigns in the UK and the USA, including the 2016 US Presidential Campaign. He is a graduate of American University and the London School of Economics and a Peace Centre fellow in Tokyo, Japan where his work is focussed on disinformation and the erosion of democracy. This is his third book and the second in the Little Black Book series.